OUTBREAK
IN
WASHINGTON, D.C.

THE 1857 MYSTERY
OF THE
NATIONAL HOTEL
DISEASE

KERRY WALTERS

THE
History
PRESS

Published by The History Press
Charleston, SC 29403
www.historypress.net

Copyright © 2014 by Kerry Walters
All rights reserved

Cover: Postcard of the National Hotel, 1907. *Courtesy of John DeFerrari.*

First published 2014

Manufactured in the United States

ISBN 978.1.62619.638.4

Library of Congress CIP data applied for.

For Michael Brown, MD
Dedicated physician & enthusiastic history buff

CONTENTS

CONTENTS

ACKNOWLEDGEMENTS

Many thanks to Kim and Jonah, to Robin Jarrell for her help with the illustrations, to Gettysburg College for the sabbatical that allowed me to write the book, to Hannah Cassilly's commissioning it as well as running down a few hard-to-locate images and to Project Editor Katie Stitely's expert guidance. Finally, thanks to Dr. Michael Brown, a physician who always livens up office visits with fascinating conversation about American history. I dedicate this little book to him.

PANIC IN WASHINGTON

It is now believed that not less than seven hundred persons have been seriously and dangerously affected by the National Hotel poison at Washington; and some twenty or thirty deaths have occurred in consequence.
—the Pennsylvanian, *May 27, 1857*

Beginning in early spring and continuing regularly through the summer of 1857, frightening rumors swept through the nation's capital and then, thanks to the still-newfangled telegraph, across the entire nation. It seemed that a mysterious malady had erupted in the National Hotel, one of the city's premier lodging establishments, not once but twice. This wouldn't have been especially newsworthy except for the fact that President-elect James Buchanan lodged at the hotel on both occasions, and that he and other dignitaries in his entourage were stricken. Buchanan was ill for months afterward, and four of his companions—a nephew, two members of Congress from Buchanan's own state of Pennsylvania and a states' rights "fire-eating" ex-governor from Mississippi—perished.

The presidential election of 1856, in which Buchanan bested two opponents, had been a particularly nasty one. The nation had been wrangling in an increasingly heated way over the issue of human bondage for years, but things had taken a dangerous turn, in 1854, with the passage of federal legislation that opened the westward territories to the expansion of slavery. The Kansas-Nebraska Act, as it came to be called, galvanized slavery's opponents as no other congressional act had, and within months, they put together a new political coalition whose

INTRODUCTION

James Buchanan, the drab career politician who became the fifteenth United States president and the most famous victim of the National Hotel disease. *Courtesy of the Library of Congress.*

members christened themselves "Republicans." A lanky lawyer from Illinois named Abraham Lincoln soon cast his lot with the coalition and vigorously campaigned for John C. Frémont, the party's first presidential candidate. Buchanan was the nominee of the Democrat Party, whose members generally favored the expansion of slavery into the territories. One of their own, Illinois senator Stephen Douglas, had actually written the Kansas-Nebraska Act. The third candidate in that 1856 race was ex-president Millard Fillmore, who ran on the American Party or Know-Nothing ticket.

The campaign rhetoric that election year boiled over with recriminations, accusations and dark insinuations that perfectly matched the angry national frame of mind. After the votes were counted and the winner decided, tempers continued to run hot. So when the news broke that President-elect Buchanan had fallen ill during his stay at the National Hotel, it was easy, given the distrustful post-election climate, for many to wonder if he had been poisoned by political enemies. That possibility alone was enough to strike horror in the hearts of some and glee in the hearts of others. Once introduced, the rumors of foul play persisted for months and, indeed, for years afterward, in some quarters. But as spring turned into summer, the poison theory gave way in most people's minds to the alternative hypothesis that a frightening disease of unknown origin had hit the National and that it could be lying in wait for the rest of Washington's citizens. The city's mayor, backed by a handful of medical authorities, did everything he could to scotch the rising panic. But for a few weeks, residents of the capital city, many of whom remembered a terrible cholera outbreak less than a decade earlier, were in a state of panic. Things only got back to normal when it became clear that the malady was limited to the National Hotel and caused,

This 1863 lithographic view of Washington from the Sixth Street Wharf is pretty much how the city looked when Buchanan was president. The unfinished Washington Monument is on the left and the Capitol dome, under construction during Buchanan's administration, is on the right. *Courtesy of the Library of Congress.*

so most of the scientific experts at the time agreed, by noxious vapors or "miasma" from backed-up sewage.

Today, the National Hotel disease, as it came to be known, is all but forgotten. The building is long gone, torn down in 1942, its old site on Pennsylvania Avenue currently home to the Newseum. The outbreak usually gets a passing nod from academic historians of this period of the nation's history, but it rarely shows up in popular histories and has never been fully explored by anyone. This is a shame for at least four separate reasons.

In the first place, the public response to the malady is a good case study of how easy it is for panic to spread. It's also yet another example of how eager people are to embrace rumors of conspiracy, often hanging on to suspicions of foul play long after it becomes clear that such suspicions simply aren't supported by the facts. Fueled by rumor, innuendo, half-truths, partisanship and incendiary journalism, distress over the origins and scope of the National Hotel disease awakened both panic and cloak-and-dagger excitement that, for a while, terrified and titillated the American public. As such, it belongs to the same lineage as the AIDS scare of the 1980s, when the origin of the disease was still undiscovered and rumors abounded that CIA-employed biologists conspired to manufacture the virus in order to target specific populations.

Moreover, the National Hotel disease deserves attention as an example of how illness can affect the ability of the nation's chief executive to perform his or her job. There are, of course, other examples from the nation's history that illustrate the fact that a sick president is a national liability. After his 1919 stroke, Woodrow Wilson was never again up to the job of running the country, and Franklin Roosevelt's shocking decline of health in the final months of his presidency has been blamed by some for his apparent willingness to make too many concessions to Soviet premier Joseph Stalin at the 1945 Yalta Conference. Similarly, it can be argued that Buchanan's judgment was clouded by the lingering effects of the National Hotel disease in the opening months of his administration, leading to at least two political blunders, surprising for a politician of his experience and temperamental caution, which tossed fuel on the flames of an already fraught national feud over slavery.

In the third place, an examination of the National Hotel disease necessarily provides an interesting—and shocking—look at the sanitation practices and policies common in American cities in the mid-1850s. At the time of Buchanan's election, Washington was a metropolis of sharp and startling contrasts. Brand-new and stately marble government buildings stood side-by-side with ramshackle hovels. Roads were unpaved, pigs and cows roamed the avenues and ponds of open sewage befouled the atmosphere in the stiflingly hot summer months. There was no public sewer system to speak of. Household waste was generally channeled through aboveground ditches to empty lots, the Potomac River or the immense and noxious canal that bisected the city. Illnesses such as cholera and dysentery weren't uncommon, especially among the poorest inhabitants. Even posh establishments like the National Hotel were generally poorly ventilated, had badly constructed water closets and were dismayingly filthy.

Finally, and perhaps most interestingly, the National Hotel disease offers a striking example of how a scrupulous medical investigation, employing the newest scientific theories and the brightest scientific minds, can be flawlessly logical but utterly mistaken. Over a period of months, individual investigators as well as boards of health weighed each piece of evidence that came to light about the possible cause or causes of the mysterious illness, rejecting them one by one until they concluded that the culprit was bad air or miasma rising from raw sewage. In doing so, they appealed to their day's most sophisticated explanation of the origin and spread of contagious diseases, an explanation that shortly, thanks to the work of luminaries such as Louis Pasteur and Robert Koch, would be replaced by the bacteria theory of disease. The medical authorities who concluded that the National Hotel disease was caused by noxious fumes were breathtakingly close to the truth; they correctly pinpointed the origin—sewage—but were unable, through no fault of their own, to understand the means of transmission. They came up with the best explanation possible at the time. But they were wrong.

This book offers the first in-depth look at the National Hotel disease. The first two chapters describe the context in which both the malady and the panic over it were generated. Chapter one looks at the presidential campaign of 1856, one in which political rivalry was so bitter that it wasn't unreasonable to presume that an attempt might have been made on the president-elect's life. Chapter two examines the dismal public sanitation of Washington at the time of Buchanan's inauguration as well as the deplorable state of the National Hotel. Chapters three and four explore the nature of the disease, its effect on Buchanan, the panic that it raised and the different theories offered at the time about its origin. Chapter five examines the tenacity with which suspicions that Buchanan had been poisoned hung on even into the twentieth century. The appendix offers selections from contemporary newspaper and journal accounts of the illness. Written by reporters covering the story, victims of the illness describing their symptoms, medical experts weighing in on the causes and editors darkly insisting that foul play was at work, the selections make for fascinating reading and give a good indication of the extent to which the National Hotel disease rattled the nation during the first half of 1857.

I
AN ACRIMONIOUS YEAR

The late Presidential election was a struggle, by one party, to discard the central idea
[of human equality], *and to substitute for it the opposite idea that slavery is right.*
—*Abraham Lincoln*[1]

American politics, especially in presidential election years, has always been a rough-and-tumble business. But in 1856, when the nation was faced with the greatest crisis since its founding, the contest for the highest elected seat in the land was especially fierce. It both reflected and aggravated deep-seated antagonisms between defenders and opponents of the "peculiar institution" of slavery, antagonisms that finally erupted in all-out war five years later. During the first half of 1857, the toxic atmosphere of distrust and suspicion bred by the national debate churned up wild rumors about the "real" nature of what happened at the National Hotel. Had there not been half a decade of escalating political feuding, there likely would have been no hubbub over the National Hotel disease.

SLAVERY AND WESTWARD EXPANSION

The United States was founded on the principle that all men were created equal. But by 1787, slavery was a legal institution in seven of the thirteen states. Persons held in bondage, nearly all of them of African origin, accounted for 18 percent of the young nation's four-million-strong population. Most of the slaves lived in the agricultural South.

Even though some whites had serious reservations about the moral propriety of slavery, for years most of them considered it a necessary evil on two counts: first, the South economically depended on it, and second, no one could quite envision what to do with the nearly 700,000 free blacks who would be produced by abolishing slavery. Partly to soothe uneasy consciences and partly to defend themselves against what they took to be northern disdain for their way of life, southerners eventually moved away from the necessary evil argument to a self-serving paternalistic one. Blacks, they insisted, were incapable of taking care of themselves. Slavery was their best chance for a decent life. So the peculiar institution evolved from being seen as a necessary evil to being defended as a positive good.

A fair percentage of northerners who disliked slavery were also willing to swallow this disingenuous defense of it. After all, slave-produced goods, particularly cotton, rice and tobacco, benefited northern manufacturers, merchants and consumers. As long as the peculiar institution was contained in the South, most northerners, even those opposed in principle to slavery, were willing to tolerate it. But what they were reluctant to accept was the expansion of slavery into the western territories held by the United States. It wasn't that they felt compassion for the plight of enslaved Africans—most whites, north and south, were openly racist—but rather that they feared land available for white settlers would be snatched up by large-scale, slave-owning plantation farmers. For most "free soilers," the name by which opponents of the westward expansion of slavery came to be called, the issue was economic rather than humanitarian.

As early as 1787, the Northwest Ordinance banned slavery in territories north of the Ohio River and east of the Mississippi River. At the time, even slaveholders were undisturbed by the ban, since few envisioned settlements ever stretching that far west. But just a generation later, westward migration had so flooded the old Northwest Territory, as well as the vast lands acquired in the 1803 Louisiana Purchase, that Congress had to broker a new policy in regards to slavery expansion. The 1820 Missouri Compromise drew an east–west line across the nation, banning slavery north of the 36° 30' parallel except in a proposed new state, Missouri. In order to maintain parity in the Senate and keep both opponents and proponents of slavery satisfied, the creation of the slave state of Missouri was balanced out by the admission of Maine as a free one.

Many congressmen and citizens genuinely believed that the Missouri Compromise would put an end once and for all to the debate about slavery's expansion. But the legislation proved unstable, with northern abolitionists so loudly and frequently condemning the very institution of slavery, not simply its expansion, that an exasperated Congress imposed a twelve-year gag rule that automatically tabled, and effectively buried, the numerous petitions for freeing the slaves regularly sent to the Capitol.

In 1845, the uneasy compromise was further rattled by the admission of a new slave state, Texas, into the Union, an act that many northern statesmen fought tooth and nail. A few months later, the United States provoked a land-grabbing war with Mexico. Upon Mexico's capitulation in 1848, the Treaty of Guadalupe Hidalgo ceded Mexican land to the United States that increased its land size by a full one-third. With this huge acquisition of territory, stretching all the way to the west coast and including all or most of what today are the states of Arizona, California, Colorado, Nevada, New Mexico, Utah and Wyoming, the debate over the westward expansion of slavery took on a new urgency.

Almost from the start of the war with Mexico, northern and southern politicians wrangled over what to do with the geographical spoils they anticipated the United States would win. In an effort to forestall southern demands for an expansion of slavery in them, a junior congressman from Pennsylvania, David Wilmot, proposed a ban on slavery in any acquired territory. The bill, known as the Wilmot Proviso, never became law. But it was reintroduced in session after session, each time igniting furious verbal and sometimes physical scuffles in the Capitol. To make matters worse, Zachary Taylor, who became president in 1849, opposed expanding slavery into the western territories, even though he was a slaveholder himself.

In an attempt to break the increasingly acrimonious impasse, Kentucky senator Henry Clay proposed a series of bills in early 1850 that he hoped would mollify, even if not totally please, both sides. After weeks of ferocious debate, during which Clay nearly abandoned hope that a compromise could be worked out, Illinois senator Stephen Douglas managed to get a modified version of Clay's bills passed that satisfied everyone just enough to avert a crisis. California would be admitted as a free state, but the immense slave state of Texas would be broken up to form two new territories, New Mexico and Utah, whose residents would decide for themselves whether they wanted slavery. The slave trade, but not slavery itself, would be abolished in Washington, D.C., but the Fugitive Slave Act, which required local magistrates and citizens to cooperate with federal marshals in pursuit of runaway slaves, would be more rigorously enforced in the North.

The president who signed the 1850 Compromise into law and who vigorously supported the Fugitive Slave Act during his time in office was Millard Fillmore, Zachary Taylor's vice president, who became chief executive when Taylor died in July 1850. The Fugitive Slave Act was extremely unpopular in the North, where many citizens refused to obey it. Fillmore's rigorous enforcement of it earned him such notoriety that his political party, the rapidly disintegrating Whigs, refused to nominate him for reelection in 1852. Instead, they chose Mexican War hero Winfield Scott as their nominee. The Democrats, for their part, settled on dark horse Franklin Pierce, who handily defeated Scott.

THE CRISIS WORSENS

Pierce's election re-stoked the debate over slavery's expansion. Although a New Englander by birth, he was a Southern sympathizer or "doughface" by conviction. As president, he fell under the influence of his party's states'-rights extremists, especially Jefferson Davis of Mississippi, who became Pierce's secretary of war. Pierce not only encouraged the adoption of slavery in the New Mexico and Utah territories but was also an enthusiastic supporter of creating slaveholding United States territories in both the Caribbean and Central America.

But none of this alienated northern free soilers, including many in Pierce's own party, as much as his support of the 1854 Kansas-Nebraska Act sponsored by fellow Democrat Stephen Douglas. Douglas proposed that the vast region of western land known as the Nebraska Territory be divided into two distinct ones, Kansas and Nebraska, and that the inhabitants of the territories be given the right to determine whether or not they wanted slavery, a doctrine known as "popular sovereignty." As precedent, he cited the 1850 agreement granting New Mexico and Utah the same right. At the same time, Douglas proposed that the Missouri Compromise agreement to limit slavery to land south of the 36° 30' parallel be declared null and void.

The Kansas-Nebraska Act eventually passed, and Pierce signed it into law. But it was a disaster for both the nation and the president's political future. Almost immediately, pro-slavers and free soilers began flooding into the Kansas Territory, each hoping to outvote the other on the issue of slavery. Predictably, both sides elected their own governors and state legislators. Pierce chose to recognize the proslavery territorial government,

Franklin Pierce, Buchanan's predecessor, who ruined his political prospects and outraged the North by signing the 1854 Kansas-Nebraska Act into law. *Courtesy of the Library of Congress.*

even though the blatant voter fraudulency with which it had been established clearly delegitimized it. Before long, the two factions each organized quasi-militias, often little more than bands of thugs and robbers, which began skirmishing with one another, especially on the Missouri-Kansas border. By the summer of 1856, "bleeding Kansas" was embroiled in a small-scale civil war. Opponents and proponents of slavery from all over the nation rallied behind one side or the other by shipping firearms, money and mercenaries to Kansas.

Early that same year, a coalition of disaffected Whigs, northern Democrats, free soilers and other opponents of the spread of slavery coalesced to form a new political party, the Republicans, whose primary purpose was to overturn the Kansas-Nebraska Act. Called "Black Republicans" by their critics, who accused them of wanting to "amalgamate" the black and white races, the members of this new party were united in their insistence that slavery had to be contained within the borders of the traditional slave states. It soon became clear that the Republicans would front a candidate in the upcoming presidential race.

THE 1856 CAMPAIGN

The two obvious contenders for the Democratic nomination in the 1856 election year were the incumbent Franklin Pierce and Illinois senator Stephen Douglas, whose sponsorship of the Kansas-Nebraska Act had made his a household name. But when the Democrats convened in Cincinnati to select a candidate, they judged both Franklin and Douglas as too hot to handle. Many northerners despised both Pierce and Douglas because of their proslavery positions, and many southerners were angry with Douglas because of his defense of popular sovereignty, believing as they did that slaveholding was a constitutionally guaranteed right, rather than something decided by popular vote. What the Democrats wanted above all was a safely electable candidate, and after seventeen ballots, they finally settled on James Buchanan. Buchanan had been in England during the acrimonious debate over Kansas-Nebraska and so was unconnected in the public mind with the whole messy affair. No one in the Democrat party was particularly enthusiastic about his candidacy—the Missouri statesman Thomas Hart Benton sourly referred to him as "never a leading man in any high sense"[2]— but neither was anyone dead set against it.

The Republicans were much more excited about their candidate: the handsome and charismatic John C. Frémont, one-time senator from California and famous explorer of the far west. Although more dashing than the drab bureaucrat Buchanan, Frémont actually had fewer qualifications for the presidency. But the Republicans counted on his celebrity status more than on his political experience to win the election.

To complicate what already promised to be an acrimonious race, a third party entered the fray. The American Party, popularly known as the "Know-

This Republican campaign poster for the 1856 presidential race features portraits of John C. Frémont and his running mate, William L. Dayton. Buchanan won the election, but he was embarrassed and outraged by the strong showing of the Republicans. *Courtesy of the Library of Congress.*

Nothings," nominated ex-president Millard Fillmore as their candidate. Theirs was essentially an isolationist party, and their platform, in addition to voicing strong anti-immigrant and anti-Catholic sentiments, demanded stringent requirements for citizenship. Democrats, on the other hand, traditionally courted the vote of immigrants, especially Irish Catholics. But on one point, Democrats and Know-Nothings were united: a Republican victory would be disastrous.

The campaign in the summer and fall of 1856 was brutal, and it coincided with an upsurge of violence in Kansas, with a proslavery mob attacking the free soil town of Lawrence and fiery abolitionist John Brown retaliating by butchering five proslavery men in what became known as the Pottawatomie Massacre. Democrats and Know-Nothings frightened the nation with hair-raising predictions that a victory for Frémont would incite more free soil violence. Additionally, it would irretrievably split the nation. The South, they argued, would never stomach a Republican as chief executive and would immediately secede. "The Union is in danger and the people everywhere begin to notice it," Buchanan proclaimed. "The Black Republicans must be, as they can be with justice, boldly assailed as disunionists, and this charge must be reiterated again and again."[3] The Democrats also played to racial prejudice by tirelessly lamenting the sweeping miscegenation they claimed a Republican victory would inaugurate, thus playing up on racial prejudice.

For their part, the Republicans countered with equally dire predictions of economic loss for white citizens if Buchanan won. They insisted that he was a spineless tool of the Slave Power who would allow slave owners to flood the western territories and snatch up all the land that otherwise could be claimed by white settlers. A campaign song written by a Republican wag quickly made the rounds.

> *No more I'm James Buchanan—I sold myself down South.*
> *Henceforth I'll do what my masters please*
> *And speak what they put in my mouth!*
> *But don't let that alarm you, forgive his slavish tone.*
> *Can you ask a man to stand up straight who was born without a backbone?*[4]

Election Day on November 4 was cold and gloomy throughout most of the North, but an astounding 83 percent of eligible voters nonetheless turned out to cast their ballots. Southerners also showed up in large numbers. When the votes were tallied, Buchanan proved the winner—but just barely. He carried fourteen slave states and five free ones, for 174 electoral votes. But his Republican opponent did surprisingly well, capturing eleven free states and 114 electoral votes. Poor Fillmore carried only Maryland, even losing his home state of New York. In raw numbers, Buchanan beat Frémont by only half a million votes, with Frémont taking a full 60 percent of the North's popular vote compared to Buchanan's 36 percent and Fillmore's 4 percent. In the South, Buchanan and Fillmore predictably took all the votes, with the Democrat at 56 percent and the Know-Nothing at 44 percent.

The presidential election of 1856 clearly demonstrated the fault line running through the nation. Normally after a national election, the tempers of the competing parties, heated to a white pitch during the campaign, cool off a bit. But the acrimony about slavery that was poisoning the nation and had made the 1856 election particularly mean-spirited escalated rather than diminished after the votes were counted. Buchanan, angered and humiliated by the fact that he'd been rejected by the majority of northerners, delivered

THE RIGHT MAN FOR THE RIGHT PLACE.

Past president Millard Fillmore entered the 1856 presidential race as a third-party candidate. This political cartoon portrays him as the only statesman who can prevent open warfare between free soilers (Frémont) and pro-slavers (Buchanan). *Courtesy of the Library of Congress.*

an astoundingly ungracious victory speech from the porch of his estate in Lancaster, Pennsylvania. "The people of the North," he complained, had foolishly chosen to support a "dangerous party"—the Republicans. Thankfully, however, the "southern people still cherish a love for the Union," and it was they who saved the day.[5]

The Republicans were also in a post-election belligerent mood. Just a month after Buchanan's victory, Abraham Lincoln, who had campaigned vigorously for Frémont, gave a speech in Chicago in which he claimed that the election of a Democrat betrayed the principle of "the equality of men." "The late presidential election," he continued, "was a struggle, by one party, to discard that central idea, and to substitute for it the opposite idea that slavery is right."

The one person with enough national stature to possibly calm the troubled waters, outgoing president Franklin Pierce, only stirred them up even more. Smarting from his own party's refusal to nominate him for a second term but unwilling to completely burn his bridges with the Democrats by lashing out at them, he turned his fury instead to the Republicans. The occasion was his final annual message, sent in December to the lame-duck Thirty-Fourth Congress.

Pierce laid responsibility for bleeding Kansas at the feet of free soilers, abolitionists and Republicans (he, like many proslavery champions, made no distinction between the three). Their "propagandist colonization" of the territory, their subversive use of "agents of disorder" and their scandalous attempts to "erect a revolutionary government" in Kansas were the sole causes of the violence there. Republicans, Pierce asserted, wouldn't be satisfied until slavery was abolished everywhere. In the pursuit of this destructive goal, they were paving the way for all-out civil war "by appeals to passion and sectional prejudice, by indoctrinating [followers] with reciprocal hatred, and by educating them to stand face to face as enemies rather than shoulder to shoulder as friends."[6] Given Pierce's close relationship with southern statesmen, especially Jefferson Davis, it's not unlikely that large portions of his incendiary message were inspired and perhaps even written by them.

If the furious Pierce's intention was to whack the hornet's nest, he succeeded. Southern congressmen immediately lauded the president's message, even though northern Democrats were a bit more reticent. Republican and free soil congressmen blasted it. Senator John Hale of New Hampshire accused the president of fomenting "hostility to the Union," and Ohio representative Lewis Campbell claimed that Pierce's message, given the turbulent and uncertain times, was a body blow that shook the nation "to its very center."[7]

Despite his petulant victory speech's denunciation of Republicans, Buchanan, after he'd calmed down a bit, recognized that the rancor over slavery had nearly reached a point of no return and that his primary task as chief executive was to "destroy any sectional party, North or South, and harmonize all sections of the Union under a national government."[8] But the discord dividing North and South, free soilers and slavers, Republicans and Democrats, was simply too strong for a man of Buchanan's cautious temperament and mediocre talents. Given the angry mood of the country, it's not surprising that rumors would soon circulate about attempts to poison him.

A CITY OF CONTRASTS

Venturing outside into the air reeking with the thick odor of the catalpa trees,
Henry Adams found himself on an earth-road, or village street, with wheel-tracks
meandering from the colonnade of the Treasury hard by, to the white marble columns
and fronts of the Post Office and Patent Office which faced each other in the distance,
like white Greek temples in the abandoned gravel-pits of a deserted Syrian city.
—Henry Adams[9]

Coming from a family that included two United States presidents and a distinguished diplomat, Henry Adams was inevitably something of an elitist. Accustomed from an early age to the finer things in life, he was bewildered and offended whenever he encountered ugliness or dissonance. As an old man, he vividly recalled a jarring example of both from his childhood. It was in the early 1850s. Stepping out of his grandmother's Washington townhouse and strolling through the capital, he was struck, even as a boy, by the incongruities he encountered: dusty avenues no more impressive than village streets randomly dotted here and there with huge buildings vaingloriously designed in the Classical style. Pretensions of civilization in the midst of a wasteland: that's how the nation's capital struck young Henry.

He wasn't alone in this judgment. Many observers of antebellum Washington, especially those who hailed from Europe, had the same impression. For them, the city was a study in contrasts. A handful of friendly visitors thought the unfinished city was charmingly full of promise. One of them, author Frances Trollope, announced herself "delighted with the whole aspect of Washington" when she visited in 1831. There was something about "the appearance of the metropolis rising gradually into life and splendor" that struck her as "a spectacle of high historic interest."[10] But when her novelist son Anthony visited Washington nearly three decades later, all he saw was a place "most ungainly and most unsatisfactory." The traveler crisscrossing the city's length on foot would soon find himself, Trollope disdainfully cautioned, needing to tuck his trousers up about his knees in order to wade through bogs and rude hillocks "out of the reach of humanity."[11]

Trollope's dismal estimation was shared by another British writer. Charles Dickens, who visited Washington during the administration of John Tyler, was equally disdainful, famously dubbing the capital the "City of Magnificent Intentions" because of its "spacious avenues, that began in nothing and lead to nowhere; streets, mile-long, that only want houses, roads and inhabitants; public buildings that need but a public to be complete; and ornaments of great thoroughfares, which only lack great thoroughfares to ornament."[12] Dickens's own government was so contemptuous of Washington's rough lack

Charles Dickens, depicted here at one of his public readings, was a less-than-impressed visitor to the nation's capital. He referred to it as a "city of magnificent intentions." *Courtesy of the Library of Congress.*

of civilization that it designated it a hardship post and awarded diplomats stationed there frontier pay.

But the French were the most biting in their criticisms of the city. One highborn mademoiselle sneered that Washington, in odd contrast to other cities, had plenty of streets but no houses.[13] The Chevalier de Bacourt complained in 1840 that the streets were unpaved, unswept and unlit, that "animals wander about all day and all night through the city," and that "women milk their cows on the sidewalk and sprinkle the passers-by. The nocturnal wandering of these beasts creates an infernal racket, in which they are joined by dogs and cats."[14] And in his famous *Democracy in America,* Alexis de Tocqueville snidely speculated that Washingtonians "conceive their public monuments on a gigantic scale" to compensate for the fact that they endure "cramped lives in tiny houses."[15]

At least one American, newspaperman George William Bagby, agreed with the foreign visitors. Washington, he wrote, is a "paradise of paradoxes…a great, little, splendid, mean, extravagant, poverty-stricken barrack."[16]

Such was the city of high ambition and low achievement inherited by James Buchanan when he was elected president of the United States. One of its best-known establishments, the National Hotel, likewise a study in contrasts, would nearly kill him.

CITY OF MAGNIFICENT INTENTIONS

The foreign and domestic sniping over the disconcertingly unfinished feel of Washington in the decades leading up to the Civil War was a bit unfair. British diplomats and French nobles turned up their noses because they inevitably compared the capital to London or Paris. But unlike these two hoary metropolises, Washington was still in its youth, barely half a century old when Buchanan took office. In fact, the plans for the city were officially presented to President Washington only in 1790, the very year of Buchanan's birth, and it took another decade before the seat of government was actually moved to the new location from New York City.

The French designer of the city, Pierre L'Enfant, envisioned it as a network of broad avenues, converging diagonally on a number of public squares and circles, which would connect public buildings grand enough to attest to the robust vitality of the new republic. At the heart of it all, built on the site's highest point, L'Enfant placed what he called "Congress House,"

Pierre L'Enfant's grand Pennsylvania Avenue connecting the Capitol and the Executive Mansion. At the start of Buchanan's administration, it was the only paved street in Washington, D.C. *Courtesy of the Library of Congress.*

an edifice Thomas Jefferson subsequently named the "Capitol." Stretching westward from Congress House, a long public park ran all the way down to the banks of the Potomac, with the "President's House," as L'Enfant called it, situated on the park's northwest corner. A long, wide boulevard to be named "Pennsylvania" would connect the two buildings.

L'Enfant's maps and architectural drawings were impressive, but the transition from blueprint to reality was strikingly less so. In superimposing the new capital onto the cluster of farms and villages (including one named Georgetown) already occupying the land earmarked for Washington, L'Enfant's perfectly geometrical grid lost something in translation. By the time Buchanan took office, the federal city looked, as a contemporary put it, "like a great lubberly lout in clothes much too large for its body and limbs."[17]

In the first place, huge open areas—fields, marshes, bogs and meadows—filled the landscape. Anthony Trollope hadn't been exaggerating by much when he insinuated that strollers through the city needed to wear a good pair of waterproof boots. Empty lots were frequently on either side of private homes and public buildings, and the farm animals that had annoyed the Chevalier de Bacourt two decades earlier still roamed. Mosquitoes swarmed by the millions from the marshes and bogs, and the excrement from all the domestic animals wandering the streets and fields both stank to high heaven and attracted armies of flies that tormented residents and visitors alike.

The capital in 1800. By Buchanan's 1856 inauguration, there was less open land, but the city was still pocked with marshes, bogs, meadows and pastures, and pigs, cows and sheep roamed free. *Courtesy of the Library of Congress.*

In the second place, the handful of public buildings that were the city's pride were mostly only half finished by the time Buchanan took office. The Capitol Building was a mass of scaffolding on his inauguration day, and had been ever since Congress agreed in 1849 to allocate funds to replace its dome and add enormous wings to either side of it. The Patent Office was still being built. The Treasury Department's massive columns hadn't yet been put into place. The General Post Office was being rebuilt. The Washington Monument, situated on the same axis as the Executive Mansion, remained incomplete and unworked on, a casualty of congressional indifference, political squabbling and a lapse in publicly subscribed funds. Its unfinished spire was not only an embarrassment—what, after all, did it say about a nation that allowed work on a monument to its founder to stall?—but it was also an eyesore, having become a favorite site for graffiti and vandalism. One of the few landmark buildings other than the President's House that actually was completed was the "Castle," finished in 1855 and housing the Smithsonian Institution.

In the third place, hovels that were homes to day laborers and free blacks often stood cheek to jowl with fine mansions and townhouses, creating an annoying eyesore for Washington's well-heeled elite and a startling

During Buchanan's administration, Washington was very much a city in progress, with federal buildings like the Post Office still under construction. *Courtesy of the Library of Congress.*

The Treasury Building, begun two years before Buchanan was sworn in as president, wasn't completed until 1869, a year after his death. *Courtesy of the Library of Congress.*

Work on the Washington Monument was stalled during Buchanan's administration due to a drop-off in public donations, making the partially constructed column a graffiti-covered eyesore. *Courtesy of the Library of Congress.*

panorama of contrast for visitors. Partly in an effort to remedy this physical mixing of the classes, real estate prices spiked sharply in the capital in the decade before the Civil War. Lots that had cost a mere four pennies per square foot in the 1840s went for a full thirty cents per square foot by the mid-1850s. Proper Washingtonians, not to mention government officials, wanted distance between themselves and the riffraff.

In the fourth place, the streets that L'Enfant had designed with such loving precision were nearly all unpaved, sending up suffocating clouds of dust in the summer and trapping pedestrians and vehicles in ankle- and axle-deep mud in the spring. There were 127 streets in Washington when Buchanan took office. Only one of them, Pennsylvania Avenue, was paved—but with such thin cobblestones that winter cold, summer rain and heavy traffic loosened many of them. Walking or riding on the long avenue was an adventure.

There was yet another factor that contributed to the sense that Washington was a lubbery lout in loose clothing: its status as a seasonal city. For part of the year, the city bustled with congressmen who arrived in the capital from all the states of the Union to conduct the nation's business. Following them to town were hucksters of every kind offering wares and services to suit all tastes. The same George William Bagby who called Washington a "paradise of paradoxes" reveled in the never-ending stream of humanity that flowed past his offices in the busy season. "Presidents, Senators, Honorables, Judges, Generals, Commodores, Governors and the Exs of all these congregate here as thick as pickpockets at a horse race. Add Ambassadors, Plenipotentiaries, Lords, Counts, Barons, Chevaliers, Captains, Lieutenants, Claim-Agents, negroes, Perpetual-Motion Men, Fire-Eaters, Irishmen, Plug-Uglies, Hoosiers, Gamblers, Californians, Mexicans, Japanese, Indians and Organ-Grinders, together with females to match."[18] But when congress adjourned, Washington emptied, and taverns, hotels, boardinghouses and streets that had been bustling with exotic figures suddenly seemed empty. Even local residents who could afford to do so left Washington in its steamy and unhealthy summer months. Then the great spaces between buildings seemed even larger and emptier. The magnificent intentions of the city's designers came across as forlorn emptiness.

CITY OF VIOLENCE

L'Enfant, a child of the Enlightenment, designed Washington to reflect the era's high esteem for reason, orderliness and uniformity. The moral corollaries of these qualities were the pillars on which the American republic claimed to rest: reason revealed the existence of natural rights to life, liberty and the pursuit of happiness; veneration for orderliness underlay the carefully contrived separation of governmental powers codified in the Constitution; and the principle of equality under the law—the equal treatment of all people—was designed to encourage a uniformity and predictability in society which mirrored that found in nature. The gleaming white marble and classical lines of the city's new public buildings were intended to symbolize these ideals of the Enlightenment.

But just as the marble was only a façade covering less glamorous brick and mortar, so the young republic's ideals of reason, orderliness and uniformity weren't always consistent with the facts on the ground. Despite what its founders hoped it would represent, Washington in the 1850s was a violent city, more often resembling a rowdy frontier town than a seat of rational and orderly republicanism.

The most dramatic evidence of the city's absence of order could be found in the halls of Congress itself. Men who were elected to the House and the Senate not uncommonly came to legislative sessions either drunk or well on their way to being so. It didn't help that both chambers periodically set out refreshment tables loaded with rum and whiskey. The loosening effects of alcohol, coupled with the growing sectional fury over slavery, led to more than one physical altercation between senators or congressmen. In the angry decade leading up to the Civil War, it wasn't uncommon for them to bring pistols and knives to chambers.

The furious debate in 1850 over the extension of slavery into the federally held territories west of the Mississippi River culminated in a confrontation in which senators Thomas Hart Benton of Missouri and Henry Foote of Mississippi nearly killed each other. After a long and increasingly heated exchange of words, a furious Benton leapt out of his seat and made for Foote, who promptly pulled a loaded and cocked pistol from his jacket and pointed it at his colleague. Benton, red-faced with rage, screamed, "Let the assassin fire! A pistol has been brought here to assassinate me!"

Fortunately, fellow senators held back Benton while others snatched the pistol from Foote's hands, and no blood was shed in the Senate on that heated day. But four years later, during the congressional wrangle over the Kansas-Nebraska Act, the incendiary piece of legislation that reawakened the debate over slavery in the territories, legislators engaged in fisticuff scuffles on the floor during debate. And two years after that, in 1856, South Carolina congressman Preston Brooks, a staunch defender of slavery and states' rights, strode over to the Senate chamber and nearly beat to death Massachusetts senator Charles Sumner, an outspoken critic of the South. Given the troubled climate of the day, it was a foolish man, as one congressman noted, who refused to carry at least a knife to the Capitol.

If the debate over slavery was a never-ending source of anger and potential violence in the halls of Congress, the actual presence of slaves in the city itself was a source of shame for many Washingtonians. More than one resident found him or herself groping for ways to respond to foreign visitors who, seeing humans in bondage for the first time, expressed outrage and disgust. The slave trade, although not slavery itself, had been eliminated in Washington in 1850. Prior to that, slave pens and markets on the Mall, not far from the Capitol itself, were both an eyesore and embarrassment, and slave coffles, long lines of shackled slaves, could be seen shuffling throughout the city, even down the main thoroughfare of Pennsylvania Avenue. The most notorious slave firm, Robey and Williams, enjoyed a thriving business; the city's location made it a convenient site for selling slaves from Virginia and Maryland. An 1835 visitor has left a horrifying portrait of the firm:

> *The outside alone is accessible to the eye of a visitor; what passes within being reserved for the exclusive observation of its owner, (a man of the name of Robey) and his unfortunate victims. It is surrounded by a wooden paling fourteen or fifteen feet in height, with the posts outside to prevent escape and separated from the building by a space too narrow to admit of a free circulation of air. At a small window above, which was unglazed and exposed alike to the heat of summer and the cold of winter, so trying to the constitution, two or three sable faces appeared, looking out wistfully to while away the time and catch a refreshing breeze; the weather being extremely hot. In this wretched hovel, all colors, except white—the only guilty one—both sexes, and all ages, are confined, exposed indiscriminately to all the contamination which may be expected in such society and under such seclusion. The inmates of the gaol [jail], of this class I mean, are even worse treated; some of them, if my informants are to be believed, having been actually frozen to death, during the inclement winters which often prevail in the country. While I was in the city, Robey had got possession of a woman, whose term of slavery was limited to six years. It was expected that she would be sold before the expiration of that period, and sent away to a distance, where the assertion of her claim would subject her to ill-usage.*[19]

By the time Buchanan took office, Robey and Williams was out of business, but nearly two thousand slaves still lived in Washington. Nearly ten thousand more free men, women and children of color also lived and worked in the city, comprising 15 percent of its total population. Some of the freedmen were skilled craftsmen or traders, but most were common laborers or domestic staff. Over half of them were illiterate, compared to an 11 percent illiteracy rate for white Washingtonians.

In many respects, the free blacks were little better off than the slaves. Washington's black laws, a set of regulations designed expressly for freedmen, were onerous. Blacks, slave or free, had to be off the streets by 10:00 p.m. In order to live in the city, free blacks had to provide proof of their freedom,

The slave trade, although not slavery, was abolished in the capital in 1850. Prior to that, the city was a thriving market for the sale and purchase of human beings, prompting antislavery broadsheets like this one from 1836. *Courtesy of the Library of Congress.*

possess letters of character written by white people and pay a hefty cash bond up front. Permission from an official magistrate was required for public gatherings of freedmen.

Although the city wasn't yet as segregated as it would become after the Civil War, most free blacks lived in houses and tenements that faced Washington's alleys, safely out of sight from the thoroughfares. The alleys were narrow, and the two- or three-storied buildings on either side allowed for little ventilation and less sunlight. The dwellings themselves, nearly all rentals, were in poor condition, broiling hot in the summer and freezing in the winter. Predictably, life in the alleys was perilous. Crime, illness and early death were normative. As an 1854 report from the city's board of health noted in speaking of death rates for children under fifteen, "much the larger proportion of these deaths are from among the children of negro, of foreign and of destitute native parents, who usually reside in alleys."[20]

The violence of slavery and poverty endured by the black community was exacerbated by the overall level of crime throughout the city. Gangs of juveniles roamed the nighttime streets—gas lamps had been introduced in 1853, but only on the busiest thoroughfares, and only lit on moonless nights—robbing and sometimes beating unfortunate wayfarers. Laborers who migrated to Washington to work on the public building projects in the summer but were idle and unemployed during the winter months, often resorted to banditry and mugging. While Congress was in session and the city was jammed with visitors, pickpockets plied their trade. Throughout winter and summer months, dozens of taverns, gambling houses and brothels, catering to black as well as white clients, contributed to the city's level of mischief. Things were so bad by 1858 that a Senate committee lamented that "Riot and bloodshed are of daily occurrence. Innocent and unoffending persons are shot, stabbed and otherwise shamefully maltreated, and not unfrequently the offender is not even arrested."[21] White-on-black crime typically went uninvestigated, as did black-on-black assaults. Moreover, the higher up the offender was on the social scale, the less likely he was to suffer legal punishment for his crime. Preston Brooks's beating of Charles Sumner earned him only a piddling fine. When United States congressman Daniel Sickles, who would lose a leg at the battle of Gettysburg, publicly shot down his wife's lover in 1859, he was speedily acquitted, prompting the editors of the *National Era* to deplore the "unparalleled depravity of Washington society."[22]

It didn't help that the Washington police force was woefully short when it came to both revenues and manpower. The city employed fifty police officers to patrol the streets by day, and the federal government paid an additional fifty to patrol at night. This meant that there was one officer for every thousand inhabitants, a ludicrous ratio when contrasted with the city of Baltimore, which employed over four hundred officers for a population much smaller than Washington's. To make matters worse, the federal police force, or "auxiliary guard," as it was called, was primarily charged with guarding standing governmental buildings from vandalism and preventing supplies from being burgled off of the city's many construction sites. The auxiliary guard had little interest in helping city cops catch run-of-the-mill criminals, and consequently, there was no love lost between the two crews. The dislike they felt for each other was nothing compared to the rivalry between the city's several volunteer fire departments, controlled by gangs whose members often fought one another with more verve than they fought fires.

CITY OF FILTH

When James Buchanan took the oath of office, there was no sewage network, no centralized garbage collection and only the initial stages of a public system of running water existed in the city that he would call home for the next four years. The privies of homes, hotels and government buildings discharged their contents into open fields or stagnant ponds, many of which were immediately adjacent to the structures themselves. Slaughterhouses likewise dumped the offal from their handiwork into the open. Residents routinely dropped slops and garbage in alleys and roadways. A succession of Washington mayors tried to enforce ordinances against the indiscriminate dumping of refuse, but to little avail. The police force was too undermanned (and probably too uninterested) to track down offenders.

The filth from raw sewage, garbage and animal intestines, coupled with the large quantities of manure dropped in city streets and alleyways by roaming pigs and cattle and horse traffic, both raised a nauseating stench that pervaded Washington during the summer months and increased the likelihood of disease. Flies and mosquitoes swarmed over the garbage and the sewage ponds. During the rainy months of spring and early summer, aboveground sewage ditches that ran into the Potomac backed up as the river rose, polluting springs from which Washingtonians drew drinking water and exposing the populace to outbreaks of dysentery, typhoid and cholera. Citywide "sanitary committees" had been established after a particularly virulent cholera epidemic in 1849. But they were as understaffed as the city police force and had a difficult time keeping abreast of all the challenges posed by the city's general lack of sanitation.

Compounding the unhealthy filthiness of the nation's capital   a squalor that stood in stark contrast to the cleanly classical architecture of its government buildings—was the fiasco of the great Washington Canal, a project that had been conceived with high hopes by the city's founders but which in reality had become little more than an enormous open cesspool. It ran just south of Pennsylvania Avenue and the President's House, more or less along the route of what is now Constitution Avenue.

The canal was planned as the primary transportation artery that would transform the fledgling city named after General Washington into a commercial powerhouse. Taking advantage of a couple creeks in the Mall region, the canal's designers dug a 160-foot-wide trench, four times the width of the Erie Canal, that connected the Potomac's east branch on the Atlantic side with its west branch. The ultimate plan was to make the Washington Canal a limb of an envisioned Chesapeake and Ohio Canal running between Georgetown and Wheeling, Virginia (now West Virginia). Goods, both imported and domestic, could then be transported from the Atlantic coast via Washington into the nation's interior. Had things worked out, the canal, which was ready for traffic by 1815, would have created great wealth for the capital city.

The canal was a disaster from the very beginning. For starters, it was too wide and too shallow. Astoundingly, the engineers who supervised its design and construction forgot the rule of thumb that narrow channels allow for a swifter flow of water than wide ones. Consequently, travel on the Canal was too sluggish to be profitable. Additionally, the water, particularly in the dry summer months, stagnated, giving rise to a foul stench and breeding disease-laden armies of mosquitoes. To make matters worse, the canal could only accommodate vessels that drew less than three feet of water. Finally, again astoundingly, the canal's locks hadn't been built with proper tidal adjustments. So when the Potomac rose, the canal often flooded, progressively building up layers of silt that clogged traffic. When the Potomac fell, the canal's water level dropped so sharply that it couldn't be used at all.

Congress regularly, albeit less and less enthusiastically, appropriated funds to deepen the canal or to dredge some of the silt out of it. By the late 1850s, it was apparent to most Washingtonians that the whole thing was hopeless. Moreover, even if the canal could have been salvaged, the steady growth of the Baltimore and Ohio Railroad, stretching all the way to the Ohio Valley, made it obsolete. Baltimore and steam beat out Washington and water transportation. Maryland's largest city, not the nation's capital, became a commercial metropolis.

When Buchanan came to Washington as president-elect, the canal had become a thing of horror that collected sewage, refuse, animal (and sometimes human) corpses and city debris, stewing them all in a toxic soup of shallow, malodorous and germ-infested water. Described by a contemporary as an "abominable sink of filth"; a "stink-trap, man-trap and mud-hole"; and a "breeder of disease and death,"[23] it was both a threat to public hygiene and a shameful eyesore. Given its location and the fetid aroma it generated, the canal was also impossible to ignore. As one historian puts it, the botched canal was "the defining feature of the midcentury downtown."[24]

An 1863 photograph of the noisome Washington Canal (right) and the disreputable Island (left), home to the recently erected Smithsonian but also brothels and gaming houses. *Courtesy of the Library of Congress.*

Cutting a path northward from the east branch of the Potomac River and making a sharp westward turn at the Capitol until it connected with the west branch of the river, the Washington Canal in effect cut off the southwestern chunk of the city from the rest. This area became known as "the Island," surrounded on all sides as it was by water. It contained the Mall, the newly built Smithsonian Institution, the United States Arsenal and the militia armory. That was the good news. The bad news was that the Island soon acquired a reputation for squalor and danger. Densely populated by free blacks and Irish immigrants, two groups whose members frequently fought with one another, the folks who lived on the Island were some of the poorest and unhealthiest in the city. Police rarely bothered to cross over the handful of bridges that connected the Island with the rest of the city to investigate robberies or assaults. Adults bathed in the filthy canal, washed their clothes in it and sometimes even drank its water. Children played and swam in it. It's not surprising that the Island had the highest infant mortality rate in the city.

The shady reputation of the Island when it came to both crime and hygiene carried over to the areas that bordered the other side of the Washington Canal. The south lawn of the President's House, called the "White Yard" because of the white picket fence that enclosed it, sloped down to the filthy

The Smithsonian Institution "Castle," completed in 1855, was the centerpiece of the city's Mall. *Courtesy of the Library of Congress.*

canal. When the rising of the Potomac caused the canal to back up and overflow, it not only created a huge disgusting sewage marsh in the low-lying island but also seeped up into the President's House grounds. Visitors and guests noted that the Executive Mansion had an ever-present foul aroma during the non-winter months. John Hay, secretary to Abraham Lincoln, Buchanan's successor, called the Executive Mansion the "White pest-house."[25] Two of Lincoln's children were chronically ill while living there. Young Willie died from typhoid fever. Although not dying, his brother Tad also came down with typhoid as well as malaria.

Pennsylvania Avenue was just to the north of the Canal and the Island. Although it prided itself on being the jewel in the city's crown, it was too close to the stench, violence and filth of the canal to escape untouched. On the north side of the avenue, the city's center market, which had been planned as a grand place of swanky stores and bustling commerce, had devolved into "an eyesore" and "the ugliest blotch on our beautiful avenue," filled with a "mean combination of ugly looking cabins" offering foodstuffs usually crawling with flies bred in the nearby canal.[26] On the avenue's south side was the city's crime-ridden red-light district known as Murder Bay, boasting over one hundred houses of ill repute that catered to every imaginable taste and added venereal diseases to the city's already impressive list of health hazards. Murder Bay was a dangerous place to venture even in the daytime. Only a foolhardy person braved it at night. A retrospective piece in the July 8, 1888 edition of the *Washington Post* provided an accurate assessment of the area:

> *The streets were unpaved, except certain of the principal thoroughfares; the houses were for the most part mean and straggling, while the moral atmosphere*

was almost in accord with the condition of the town itself. Gambling establishments, some of the highest order, and descending by gradations to dens of the lowest character, where life itself was frequently sacrificed on the turning of a card. Thieves and unprincipled men and women, as ready to cut a throat as pick a pocket, flourished and walked the streets in certain sections in open daylight, while at night they frequented the haunts of vice and selected their victims from among the unsophisticated without fear of law or justice. In those sections it was unsafe for any one [sic] with the slightest appearance of respectability to enter after nightfall. There were, of course, the respectable sections, and numbers of people lived here and mingled in society who knew little or nothing of the darker localities, except as they were brought to their attention through the newspapers; but to the people who saw down-town life, as it may be termed, after the town was buried in darkness, except for the straggling rays from dim street lamps or the light from the saloons and gambling places, Washington was a wild and weird place.

THE NATIONAL HOTEL

By far the toniest part of the city, despite the "blotch" of the center market between Seventh and Ninth Streets, was north Pennsylvania Avenue, not the least because that's where many of the city's bustling hotels were located. In the first half of the nineteenth century, Washington's most lucrative and respectable business—besides governance—was providing accommodations for the elected officials, many of them with families in tow, who descended on the city when Congress was in session. No less a person than George Washington himself built the first boardinghouse in the capital, intending it as an encouragement for citizens of the new nation to run for office, even though doing so might mean forsaking the comforts of home for months on end. At least, Washington hoped, they would have decent and comfortable living quarters for their pains. He situated his hostelry near Capitol Hill.

It wasn't long before others in the city emulated General Washington by building additional seasonal boardinghouses, and not long after that the hotels along Pennsylvania Avenue began to go up. The hotels, many of them quite grand affairs, quickly became the city's social centers, serving gargantuan meals several times a day and housing bars loaded with unending supplies of liquor and beer to quench the thirst of politicians whose throats had grown dry from orating in the chambers of Congress. Noisy crowds of locals, eager to discuss the news and gossip of the day, filled hotel bars, parlors and lounges, often to the dismay of foreign visitors. The British guests in particular disdained the hotels for their noise, their tobacco-stained carpets—spittoons were strategically placed but seldom used by tobacco and snuff users—and the gluttonous eating and drinking that went on in them. Lord Lyons, the British minister to Washington from 1858 to 1865, complained that in addition to the city's lack of good clubs, restaurants, opera and theater, the hotel accommodations were execrable. But native evaluations of the hotels were much friendlier. William D'Arcy Haley's 1860 guidebook to the capital was typical: "The hotels of Washington have submitted to a great amount of undeserved abuse from abroad, but they present more features of interest than any similar establishments in the country; for here you meet, not only those who come to buy and sell, and to discuss the rise or fall of stocks, but those whose traffic is with national affairs."[27]

The steady stream of traffic in and out of the hotels, whether visitors to the capital city who sought lodgings in them or locals who noisily congregated in their dining rooms and saloons, offered ample opportunity for scam artists, and hotel proprietors frequently warned their clientele to be on guard against common pickpockets and thieves on the one hand and flimflam artists posing as congressmen or entrepreneurs on the other. In addition to the crooks and scalawags that the hotels attracted, many of them also soon acquired their share of eccentric hangers-on who, while innocent enough, were adept at finagling a meal or drink from hotel guests. One of the more famous of them was "Colonel" Beau Hickman, who for nearly forty years, beginning in the 1840s, was a fixture in Washington's hotels. As a young man, Hickman had squandered a considerable fortune (or at least so legend had it). Undaunted by his reduced circumstances, he haunted the city's fashionable spots. Armed with fashionable beaver hat, diamond stick pin, cane and exquisite manners, this perennial dandy was always ready to play a game of cards or serve as a guide for visitors. He lived off the kindness of strangers until his death in 1873 and was memorialized six years later in a pamphlet affectionately entitled *The Life and Anecdotes of Beau Hickman, Prince of the Bummers.*

Hickman could be found in the parlors and bars of all of Pennsylvania Avenue's swankiest hotels: Willard's on the corner of Fourteenth Street and Pennsylvania; Brown's, sometimes called the Indian Queen because of the picture of Pocahontas on its sign; the Kirkwood House on the corner of Twelfth and Pennsylvania; the Saint Charles; or the Washington. His home base, the hotel in which he himself lodged and most often held court, was the National, located about halfway between the Capitol and the President's House, an easy walk to the First Baptist Church of Washington on whose site Ford's Theater would be erected in 1863. (John Wilkes Booth preferred the National to all other hotels and lodged there in the days before he assassinated President Lincoln.)

The city's first-class hotels energetically competed for the status of being the single best that the city had to offer. But most observers agreed that Willard's and the National were the two most often in a dead heat for that honor. Some seasons Willard's came out first; in others, the National was the place to lodge and be seen. But throughout the 1850s, the National usually took pride of place, particularly among southern-born congressmen. Kentucky senator Henry Clay, one of the truly great statesmen of his generation, boarded there for years, eventually dying at the National in June 1852. In all likelihood, his residency there is why an enormous crowd gathered at the hotel after the 1850 Compromise saved the Union to listen to the Marine Band and hear speeches from Clay, Daniel Webster, Sam Houston and Stephen Douglas, each of whom had played a hand in drafting the compromise and getting it through Congress. An 1860 guidebook to Washington was effusive in its praise of the establishment.

The National Hotel is the largest hotel in the city, and one of the largest in the country. It is situated on Pennsylvania avenue, at the corner of Sixth street, and occupies the entire depth of the block. The old National is the stamping-ground of politicians and the grand centre of political intrigue.

The Indian Queen Hotel, one of the posh Pennsylvania Avenue establishments, was a competitor of the National Hotel. *Courtesy of the Library of Congress.*

Its crowded halls and gay saloons and parlors are proverbial among old frequenters of the seat of government, while its proximity to the Capitol, and excellent management, render it the most favored hotel in Washington.[28]

The National's history began before it was even named. In 1816, Roger Weightman—businessman, veteran of the War of 1812, philanthropist and one-time mayor of Washington—constructed six Federal-style row houses on the corner of what's now 6th Street and Pennsylvania Avenue. Ten years later, he sold them to John Gadsby, a British-born entrepreneur who operated a tavern in Alexandria (Gadsby's Tavern is still operating) and a hotel in Baltimore (where he became the city's largest slave owner) before relocating to Washington. Gadsby hired carpenters to link the row houses together to form the city's largest hotel, boasting some two hundred rooms. Although for years afterward the place was often called "Gadsby's," its official name was the National Hotel. To emphasize the establishment's patriotic name, Gadsby timed the grand opening to coincide with George Washington's birthday. Everyone who was anyone, including President John Quincy Adams, attended.

In an era when Washington's hotels were noted for their generous menus, the National was especially famous for both the abundance of its fare and the unusual way Gadsby insisted it be presented to guests. Probably in keeping

A late-nineteenth-century montage of the capital's train station and most famous hotels. The huge National Hotel is given pride of place at the bottom center. As the National's reputation declined after the outbreak, that of Willard's Hotel, bottom right, rose. *Courtesy of the Library of Congress.*

John Gadsby, the British entrepreneur who built the National Hotel, started out as the owner of Gadsby's Tavern in Alexandria. The tavern is still a working establishment. *Courtesy of the Library of Congress.*

with the establishment's "national" theme, meals were served up in quasi-military style. One 1820s visitor to the hotel's vast dining room left a vivid description of the spectacle:

> *The guests being all seated, and an army of colored servants standing behind the chairs, Mr. Gadsby, a short, stout gentleman, standing at the head of the table, the guests silent with expectation, the word was given, "Remove covers!" when all the servants moved like automata, each at the same moment placing his hand upon the handle of a cover, each at the same instant lifting it, stepping back in line and facing to the head of the table, and, at a sign from Mr. Gadsby, all marching and keeping regular step to the place of depositing the covers, and then back, to commence waiting on the guests.*[29]

When Gadsby died rich in years and possessions in 1844, his heirs sold the hotel. The new owners promptly enlarged it in both width and height, stretching the edifice over an entire city block. But the additions were poorly designed and haphazardly built, and the National Hotel that emerged was dark, ill-ventilated and easy to get lost in. Fifteen years later, in the wake of the mysterious disease that struck down guests, the mayor of Washington would chide the hotel owners for the building's unhealthily cramped quarters that trapped noxious aromas rising from the numerous water closets.

> *The hotel was not built upon any pre-conceived and well-arranged plan, but has been several times extended and otherwise altered, so that it has been impossible to adopt or carry out any regular system of ventilation. Indeed that object, important as it is, seems to have been almost entirely lost sight of, and with many of the old flues, with their registers, placed in the building to conduct the heated air through it, have been suffered to remain, though the method of heating the house has been changed; and they serve as conduits through which mephitic* [pestilential] *gases were conveyed all over the house.*[30]

It wasn't just the hotel's ventilation that was "mephitic." Despite its prestige as a luxury establishment that catered to the very best of Washington society, the National also had a reputation for being dirty. Perhaps its lack of cleanliness was the inevitable result of its sprawl and confusing labyrinth of dark nooks and crannies. Perhaps in a city already noteworthy for its fetid marshes and disgusting canal, its swarms of flies and mosquitoes and its open-air dumps, the dirtiness of the National didn't strike its proprietors as out of the ordinary. But more than one guest was shocked and dismayed by the grime. Even after the hotel tried to rehabilitate itself in the wake of the outbreak that laid Buchanan low by scrubbing everything down from top to bottom and replacing worn-out furniture, guests remarked on its general filthiness. Seven years later, the wife of a Union general who had taken a room at the National stormed out in disgust, telling anyone who would listen that she hadn't the grit to endure such disgusting accommodations.[31]

So the National Hotel, like the city in which it was situated, was a study in vivid contrasts. It served sumptuous meals prepared, as would become clear when the disease named after it struck, in filthy kitchens. It prided itself on being the largest hotel in Washington but apparently gave little thought to proper ventilation. It employed a small army of servants but had a reputation for sloppy housekeeping. And in 1857, it acquired the dark distinction of poisoning the single most important man in the entire nation: President-elect James Buchanan. It was a blot on the hotel's reputation that it never quite managed to erase.

III

A STRICKEN PRESIDENT-ELECT

We were somewhat fearful that Mr. Buchanan might be seriously embarrassed during the inaugural ceremonies by the effects of what was then known as the National Hotel disease.
—James Buchanan Henry[32]

The weather was atrocious the day before and would turn frigid again the day after. But when James Buchanan became the nation's fifteenth president on March 4, 1857, the temperature rose, astoundingly, to the mid-sixties. The thousands of visitors who had crammed into the capital to witness the "glorious festivities," as that day's edition of the *Washington Evening Star* called Buchanan's inauguration, were delighted at the unexpected shift in the weather.

The inaugural procession to the Capitol and the swearing-in started at noon. Buchanan's friend General John Quitman of Mississippi, dressed in a crisp new uniform and riding on a splendid steed, led three hundred Marines and several companies of states militia down Pennsylvania Avenue. Marching behind them was a handful of grizzled veterans from the War of 1812 who were greeted with wild huzzahs from the crowd lining both sides of the avenue. Also in the parade, for the first time ever in a presidential inauguration, were floats. One of them, the "Goddess of Liberty Car," featured a woman dressed as the goddess seated next to a fifty-foot pole bearing the stars and stripes. Another float was a replica of the frigate USS *Constitution*, so large that sailors entertained the crowd by climbing in its rigging as the float, drawn by several teams of sturdy horses, lumbered along.

Buchanan's inaugural parade, which stretched for blocks down Pennsylvania Avenue, was the first to have floats. The largest was a replica of the USS *Constitution* that was so large that sailors could climb in its rigging. *Courtesy of the Library of Congress.*

When the procession was only a few blocks from the Capitol, it halted in front of the National Hotel, where a large four-horse barouche joined it. Seated in the carriage were the outgoing president, Franklin Pierce, and the president-elect, James Buchanan. As the parade recommenced and the crowd saw the two men, a roar went up that continued all the way to the Capitol. Buchanan and Pierce climbed down from the barouche, entered the building between two lines of uniformed and saluting soldiers and were escorted to a room to await the swearing-in of the vice president-elect, John C. Breckinridge of Kentucky. (Protocol demanded that the vice president be sworn in before the president.)

Finally, at around 1:45 p.m., Buchanan made his way to the inaugural platform, followed by President Pierce, members of the Supreme Court, senators and representatives and finally the gaudily beribboned diplomats of a dozen nations. Army captain Montgomery Meigs, a brilliant young engineer who would serve as quartermaster general for the Union during the Civil War, had been put in charge five years earlier of supervising the construction of the Capitol building's new wings and dome. The project was still ongoing—in fact, scaffolding for erecting the dome had only just been put up—and huge slabs of raw marble lay in the yard in front of the eastern portico. Worried

Right: Army engineer Montgomery Meigs (pictured here as quartermaster general during the Civil War), was commissioned to add wings and a new dome to the Capitol. The work was still in progress during Buchanan's inauguration. *Courtesy of the Library of Congress.*

Below: The resourceful Meigs had marble paneling that was stacked in front of the unfinished Capitol covered in wooden planks to protect it from the inaugural crowds. Afterwards, he used the wood for scaffolding. *Courtesy of the Library of Congress.*

Between five thousand and six thousand people crammed into the building that housed Buchanan's inaugural ball to dine on a many-coursed banquet and dance until dawn. *Courtesy of the Library of Congress.*

about the thousands of inaugural spectators scuffing and chipping the stone, Meigs had the blocks covered by a wooden casing, the timber from which the ever-practical engineer planned to use afterward for additional scaffolding.

Once on the platform, Buchanan removed his hat and bowed again and again to the crowd's acclaim. He delivered an inaugural address that was audible to only those standing closest to the platform, and then Chief Justice Robert B. Taney administered the oath of office. It was the sixth time that the aged Supreme Court head had sworn in a chief executive. He would do so for a final time four years later on Abraham Lincoln's inauguration day.

As at all presidential inaugurations, the rest of the day and night was packed with dances, dinners, receptions, drinking and sometimes riotous merrymaking. The National Inaugural Ball was held in a specially built wooden building, 235 feet long, 56 feet wide and 20 feet high. Its walls were draped with red, white and blue crepe, and dozens of chandeliers lighted the room. By the time President Buchanan made an appearance at around 11:00 that night, there were so many people—five thousand to six thousand—jammed shoulder to shoulder inside that dancing was impossible. Supper, served in a separate building, featured four hundred gallons of oysters, 1,200 quarts of ice cream, eight hundred chickens, sixty saddles of mutton and seventy-five hams. After saying a few words to the assembled revelers, the president left the ball shortly after midnight, even though guests remained to eat, drink, chatter and—when the crowd thinned—dance until 4:00 in the morning.

Although a few newspaper editors hostile to the Democrats sniffed at the inauguration—*Harper's Weekly* for March 14, 1857, sourly called it a "somewhat tawdry" affair that reeked "terribly of monarchical example and American apishness"—most judged the day a spectacular success. Their high spirits would have been tempered had they known that Buchanan hadn't been sure he would make it through the day. He was violently sick from something he'd picked up five weeks earlier. As his nephew and secretary James Buchanan Henry recalled years afterward, "We were somewhat fearful that Mr. Buchanan might be seriously embarrassed during the inaugural ceremonies from the effects of what was then known as the National Hotel disease." In fact, the president-elect was so ill during his inauguration that he insisted that a naval surgeon, Dr. Jonathan M. Foltz, attend him both during the ceremony and for several weeks thereafter. Buchanan was convinced that he had managed to hold up during his inaugural speech only because of the small doses of brandy with which Foltz settled down his churning stomach and bowels and fortified his resolve.

It was a bad way to start a presidency.

"WHY, I HAVE BEEN POISONED!"

The affliction that some newspapers dubbed "the Buchanan grip" but that most came to call the "National Hotel disease" hit Buchanan in late January 1857 as he was trying to cope with the avalanche of office-seeking petitions that inevitably buried presidents-elect in the nineteenth century.

Buchanan's pre-inauguration woes were compounded by the unhappy fact that he was having some difficulty holding his party together. Pennsylvania Democrats had declined to elect his old friend and supporter John Weiss Forney to the Senate, despite the fact that the president-elect had made his desire to see Forney so placed more than clear. Moreover, southern and northern Democrats, beginning to pull in opposite directions on the slavery issue, were increasingly suspicious of one another. Putting together a presidential cabinet that satisfied both groups was proving harder than Buchanan had anticipated. Finally, Stephen Douglas of Illinois, who had competed with Buchanan for the Democratic nomination the previous year, had allied himself with powerful Mississippi statesman Jefferson Davis to lobby for the appointment of Michigan senator Lewis Cass to head the State Department. The problem was that Buchanan couldn't stand Cass.

The situation grew so tense in the weeks following the election that one of Buchanan's cronies, Senator John Slidell from Louisiana, finally urged him to leave his Wheatland estate in Lancaster, Pennsylvania, and travel to the nation's capital to smooth the ruffled waters. "You will of course be immensely annoyed," he told Buchanan, "but…you cannot correctly feel the public pulse anywhere else."[33] So the president-elect reluctantly made plans to leave the comfort of his home and go to Washington.

The trip was delayed a few days because of an arctic blast that swept the country from upper Michigan to Baltimore and Bangor to Dubuque. The snow fell in buckets, closing down rail and carriage traffic throughout the northeast and middle-Atlantic states, and at their worst, temperatures dropped to forty degrees below zero. One Washington newspaper that had gotten word Buchanan was coming to town announced that the weather had forced him to cancel his visit.[34] But the notice was incorrect. Buchanan, determined to brave the frigid temperatures, left Lancaster on January 26, stopped overnight in Baltimore and arrived in Washington the next morning. Since no one was expecting him, there was no fanfare at the train station. Buchanan and the friends who accompanied him jumped into a cab and made their way to the National Hotel, whose manager, John Guy, was a fellow Lancastrian and old acquaintance.

Details about Buchanan's stay in the capital are a bit hazy. The *Pennsylvanian,* a newspaper edited by his friend John Weiss Forney, the man whom Buchanan had unsuccessfully lobbied to get into the Senate, reported that he declined dinner invitations from both President Pierce and Senator Douglas. Others, however, reported that Buchanan did dine with them and other notables on at least two different occasions during his visit. He also met with Democrat cronies in an effort to put an end to the intraparty squabbling.

What seems pretty definite is that Buchanan and his traveling companions took at least one meal at the National Hotel. Jonathan Foltz, the physician who kept Buchanan on his feet during the inauguration, happened to have been a guest at Wheatland when the president-elect decided to go to Washington, and he accompanied him there. Foltz recalled that the party of nine, weary from their journey, ate at the National on the evening of their arrival. They all retired around 10:00 p.m. Two hours later, Foltz awoke, so violently ill that his first thought was, "Why, I have been poisoned!"[35]

Taking no chances, Foltz immediately reached in his doctor's bag for an emetic, and "by vigorous measures," as his biographer delicately puts it, managed to empty the contents of his stomach. He had scarcely finished this unpleasant task when a hotel servant began pounding on his door to tell him that Buchanan was sick and in need of the doctor's services. Foltz rushed to the president-elect's room to find him "very ill indeed,"[36] suffering in the same way the doctor had earlier, and it wasn't long before all but two of Buchanan's traveling companions required Foltz's ministrations as well. He was up the rest of the night running from room to room, helping the stricken guests purge themselves as best they could.

The next day, Buchanan and his unlucky companions were too sick to leave their beds. In trying to piece together the cause of their illness, Foltz eventually concluded that it was the soup they had taken at supper the night before. The two men in the company who didn't sicken hadn't eaten any of it, and Foltz, who was the least ill of those stricken, had taken but little.

The symptoms endured by all the men were similar: diarrhea, loss of appetite, cramping in the stomach and bowels and bellies swollen by flatulence. The diarrhea was explosive and of a frothy or yeasty appearance. There was some nausea that worsened to the point of convulsive vomiting if the diarrhea was checked by astringents. The diarrhea and the vomiting quickly dehydrated the sick men, and they all suffered greatly from thirst. But the liquids they were given went straight through them, doing little to hydrate them.

By January 29, the worst seemed over, and the men had recovered enough to leave their beds. As they gathered that morning for toast and cups of weak tea, they joked about their malady and, thinking they were cured, forgot about it. Buchanan spent the rest of his time in Washington trying to mend political fences and making the social rounds. He was apparently well enough on the evening of Saturday, January 31, to attend a soirée at the Executive Mansion and one the following night hosted by Mrs. Stephen Douglas. He departed for home on February 3, in weather so bad that one Pennsylvania newspaper reported that the president-elect "footed it" the last ten miles to Wheatland, a feat that suggests how much he had recovered from his indisposition.[37]

Once back home, Buchanan returned to the business of sorting out his cabinet, putting up all the while with a continuous stream of visitors. Over the next three weeks, he managed to select candidates for all but two cabinet positions. One of them went to Lewis Cass. Buchanan liked him no better than he ever had, but he realized that political expediency required the senator's appointment. And then, on February 25, Buchanan published a surprising note in several newspapers announcing that he would receive no more visitors until after the inauguration. The doors of Wheatland were closed.

It was an odd notice that put reporters on the alert that something was amiss. Although Buchanan wasn't an especially warm man, he enjoyed having people around him. The president-elect's handlers tried to spin the story to his advantage: Buchanan sought seclusion to work on his inaugural speech; Buchanan needed peace and quiet to finish making his cabinet selections; Buchanan required some downtime to rest up after the hectic weeks of politicking that followed his election. Doubtlessly there was a bit of truth to each of these claims. But outweighing all of them was the fact that the affliction that had struck Buchanan at the National Hotel in late January had returned with a vengeance. In the days leading up to and including his inauguration, the president-elect was a very sick man. And that was a fact neither Buchanan nor his advisors wanted to see trumpeted in the press.

Dr. Foltz was called back to Wheatland on February 24 after being "informed that Mr. Buchanan had a severe relapse…and was quite unwell"[38] and proceeded to treat the same symptoms that had laid the traveling party low at the National Hotel nearly a month earlier. He was surprised at the recurrence of the malady, since he, along with the others, had assumed that the affliction was over and done. One of the curiosities of the disease was its persistent refusal to go away. Other persons stricken with it would suffer intermittently with diarrhea, cramps and nausea over periods that involved months and, in a few cases, years. The symptoms would disappear, giving the patient a false confidence, only to resume, seemingly arbitrarily, at a future date. In the final days of February, Buchanan experienced his first relapse.

RETURN TO THE NATIONAL HOTEL

Foltz continued to suspect that the National Hotel's soup was the culprit, and as the president-elect's physician, he warned him against returning to the establishment for the inauguration. But Buchanan ignored the advice. His temperamental reserve meant that he was a man with few friends. But he was fiercely loyal to the ones he had, and in all probability, he made the decision to stay at the National again because he was worried that word of his illness would leak out and damage the interests of the hotel's manager, his old acquaintance from Lancaster. So he announced that he would once again lodge at the hotel until he moved into the Executive Mansion.

The president-elect and a large party of relatives, friends and aides set out for Washington on the cold and snowy morning of March 2. The day was so cold that Lancaster bandsmen who had congregated to give Buchanan a musical sendoff soon threw in the towel and hurried back indoors. Buchanan and his party had to switch trains in Baltimore, and a huge crowd of supporters as well as an equally large crowd of hecklers came out to greet or hoot him. Buchanan was nearly oblivious to it all. He was so ill that he bowed out of a celebratory banquet hosted by the city's mayor, collapsing instead in a hotel room until it was time to leave for the nation's capital.

Buchanan was checked into the National for two days and two nights, although it's not clear that he spent much time there. (Even so, the hotel ran up an American flag as a proud announcement that the president-elect was a guest.) He may have spent at least one of the nights before his inauguration with the Washington banker and art collector William Wilson Corcoran. He conducted business in the National during the days, but it's not clear that he ate anything there more than crackers, and he attended a pre-inaugural ball hosted at the National. Although Buchanan didn't want to hurt his friend's business, he apparently saw no need to take a chance by eating his food. Besides, he was ill enough as it was and constantly in need of Dr. Foltz's doses of anti-diarrheal medication and brandy.

The National was crammed with people, many of them dignitaries, who had traveled to Washington for the inauguration. A good number of them, especially those whose rooms were above the first floor, noticed a disgusting aroma that reminded them of sewage. But it was only when dozens of the guests fell ill with the same symptoms that had floored Buchanan and his traveling companions at the end of January that the newspapers began to take notice. Word soon got out that Buchanan had been stricken earlier, and the natural assumption made by both reporters and the general public was that his second stay at the hotel had made him ill again. In all likelihood, however, he was suffering a relapse rather than a fresh exposure to the cause of the malady.

Within a week of the inauguration, Washington was abuzz with alarming stories about the strange illness afflicting National Hotel guests. By mid-month, newspapers were giving their readers regular reports on the affair, and by the month's end, victims of the National Hotel disease, as it was now most commonly called to the dismay of the hotel owners, were writing letters to newspapers describing their ordeals. In an age in which reporters and editors were more than content to pass on unverified rumors as news, exaggerations about the intensity and scope of the malady soared. It's impossible at this date to know with any precision the numbers of people affected, much less those who actually died. But at the time, estimates improbably ran into the hundreds. As early as March 21, the *New York Daily Herald* quoted one victim who claimed that nearly one hundred of the hotel's guests were sickened. The *Pennsylvanian* for May 27 improbably estimated that "no less than seven hundred" people were affected. Years afterward, long after the National Hotel disease was nothing but a memory, estimates of the disease's casualties continued to be exaggerated. Looking back on the affair, Dr. Foltz insisted that upward of four hundred people were infected, with a 10 percent mortality rate.[39]

BUCHANAN'S HEALTH

By April and May, the press had gone into overdrive in its reportage of the National Hotel disease, taking obvious delight in describing its symptoms and its victims and, in the process, whipping up anxiety and sometimes panic in its readers. But what generally wasn't reported was the fact that President Buchanan remained sick for weeks after his inauguration. He was attended round the clock by the loyal Dr. Foltz and did his best to perform his presidential duties. But he was ill, both from the recurring symptoms of the National Hotel disease and from the generally poor state of his health.

That Buchanan wasn't a particularly healthy man, even before he fell victim to the National Hotel disease, wasn't widely known or reported. In fact, many journalists covering the inauguration commented on his healthy, robust appearance, despite the fact that he was sixty-five years old. (Only two other United States presidents, William Henry Harrison before him and Ronald Reagan after him, were older when they took the oath of office.) Observers were deceived by the fact that Buchanan stood six feet—he appeared even taller because he tended to comb his mane of white hair straight up—and had the ruddy complexion that the people of his day took as a mark of good health. Moreover, despite the fact that a defect of vision caused him to hold his head to one side and squint, he generally carried himself well, standing erect with chest thrown out. Additionally, he was, by all accounts, light on his feet, with an elastic, almost bouncy, step. In short, he exuded the appearance of wellness.

In reality, as one of his biographers put it, "he was plagued by bad health."[40] Buchanan suffered most of his life from what nineteenth-century medicine referred to as "biliousness." He was regularly laid low by violent episodes of headache, nausea and vomiting when he was anxious and was so often ill during the presidential campaign that he had to keep a slop bucket close at hand. Earlier in life he had endured two serious and painful operations, one for polyps in his nose and another on his neck for unspecified glandular problems that left severe scarring, which Buchanan ever afterward tried to hide by wearing high collars. By the time he was elected president, he had also picked up a heart problem, and the gout that would plague him in his retirement had already made an appearance. Under the immaculate and almost clerical black suits that he habitually wore, his body was puffy and fleshy; although he carried it well, he was overweight. To top off all his problems, Buchanan was one of the heaviest drinkers to hold the presidency. Both his acquaintances and the press marveled at the amount of liquor and wine he was capable of consuming in a sitting, as well as in the fact that he never seemed drunk or even more than slightly tipsy. Nor was Buchanan an occasional imbiber. At least one report had him going through two bottles of hard liquor a day. As one of his friends noted, probably without much exaggeration, "The madeira and sherry that he had consumed would fill more than one wine cellar."[41] It's not surprising that brandy was one of the "medications" with which Dr. Foltz fortified Buchanan to get him through inauguration day.

Given the state of Buchanan's overall health, the National Hotel disease hit him especially hard. His nausea, diarrhea and general fatigue prompted him to keep Dr. Foltz at the President's House, so he would be close by when things got bad, for several weeks after the inauguration. Foltz apparently wasn't eager to remain, but Buchanan lured him with promises of a high governmental position. (Buchanan never delivered, and a disappointed Foltz, who had been devoted to Buchanan, eventually turned against him.) Even after Foltz finally left the Executive Mansion, he periodically dropped by to appraise his patient's condition. The summer following the inauguration, he noted that on one of these visits, "I found [Buchanan] much altered. There are those who are daily praying that he may be removed that the Vice-President may take his place. I am not so vain as to suppose that I could arrest such an event, but perhaps I could assist to avert it."[42] A month earlier, the *Columbus Enquirer* reported on May 5 that "a very distinguished democrat, just from Washington, expresses to us the opinion that Mr. Buchanan will not live much longer." Buchanan, the source said, was suffering from "the labors of the office" and the "tremendous pressure of office-seekers." But "the disease contracted by [the president] at the National Hotel appears to be hastening his inevitable fate."

For the first few weeks of his residency in the Executive Mansion, President Buchanan was so ill from the National Hotel disease that he insisted his personal physician, Dr. Jonathan Foltz, reside with him. *Courtesy of the Library of Congress.*

OFF HIS GAME

At least one historian has considered the possibility that Buchanan's undermined physical health may have affected his judgment and performance in the first months of his administration.[43] As a politician, Buchanan was a survivor with a long track record of playing it safe. Temperamentally, he was a somewhat petulant man, easily offended by disagreement and prone to sulkiness when crossed. But he was also timid and indecisive, and had lasted in national politics for four decades by laying low. He learned early on to hide his pique, lest it bring him enemies, and to avoid direct confrontation with political adversaries. Only once in his long career as a congressman, senator, ambassador and secretary of state did "Old Public Functionary," as he was disdainfully called by his enemies, find himself in the middle of a ruckus. While serving as ambassador to the Court of Saint James, Buchanan co-authored a policy memorandum, the so-called Ostend Manifesto, which outlined a strategy for the acquisition of Cuba. President Pierce, a southerner in sympathy although a New Englander by birth, wanted to acquire the plantation island to appease the slave-holding South, and instructed Buchanan to recommend a way to go about it. In the manifesto, Buchanan suggested that if cash-strapped Spain wouldn't agree to sell Cuba, the United States would be perfectly warranted in seizing it by force. "By every law human and Divine," he wrote, "we shall be justified in wresting it from Spain."[44] Unfortunately, the memo was leaked to the press, and its unabashed endorsement of manifest destiny and the extension of slavery created an uproar, especially in antislavery circles. Buchanan caught a bit of heat for his participation in its drafting. But characteristically, he had anticipated such a possibility and provided a way out for himself by making it clear in the manifesto's very first line that it was "written in compliance with the wish expressed by the President."[45] Once again, Old Public Functionary had played it safe.

Given his political style, the post-election decisions President Buchanan made, both before and after his swearing-in, are surprising. They reveal a public display of irritability and impatience uncharacteristic of the man, as well as an unusually passive subservience, extreme even in a play-it-safe politician like Buchanan, to party powerbrokers. It's not unreasonable to wonder whether Buchanan's decisions were influenced, at least in part, by the state of his health. Chronic diarrhea, nausea, stomach cramps and lassitude are not only psychologically distressing, especially for someone in the public eye like the chief executive, but also physically wearying. The presidency is a hard job. Under the best of circumstances, chief executives sometimes make bad calls. But for a man already in weak health who suffers from a chronic and debilitating malady, the odds of making hasty decisions and poor judgments increase exponentially. Buchanan is generally—and accurately—reckoned by historians to be one of the worst presidents ever to occupy the White House. In terms of talent, intelligence and personality, he was simply the wrong man for the job in the fraught years leading up to civil war. But his performance might well have been made poorer by physical debility during his first months in office.

Two blunders of colossal proportion suggest that Buchanan was off his game: his mishandling of the Dred Scott Supreme Court case and the uncompromisingly antagonistic tone of his inaugural address.

Dred Scott v. Sandford, which generated one of the most infamous decisions ever to be handed down from the highest bench in the nation, had been moving through the courts since 1846. The plaintive, a Virginia-born slave named Dred Scott, argued that he was a de facto free man because his master had relocated with him to the free states of Illinois and Wisconsin. Consequently, it was a violation of Scott's rights for him (or his family) to be held as slaves. His case was strengthened by the fact that at least one lower court (in Missouri) had ruled several times that slaves whose owners had taken them to free states or territories were, by virtue of that, free.

Both advocates and opponents of slavery closely watch the case; both sides sensed that the court's ruling would be a landmark in the increasingly acrimonious national debate over human bondage. President-elect Buchanan knew that the southern-dominated court was likely to rule against Scott. But, more ready than usual to kowtow to the southern wing of his party, he didn't want the decision to look sectional. So he

Possibly because his judgment was impaired by illness, Buchanan illegally meddled with the Supreme Court case of *Dred Scott v. Sandford*. The judgment, which denied that blacks like Dred Scott were citizens with rights, fueled the growing debate about slavery. *Courtesy of the Library of Congress.*

secretly wrote Justice Robert Grier, a fellow Pennsylvanian, urging him to vote in line with the majority of his judicial colleagues. Buchanan's solicitation was utterly improper and likely illegal, but it worked. Grier agreed, and the decision, announced two days after Buchanan took the oath of office, went against Scott, with only two dissenting opinions. Chief Justice Taney, who wrote the majority opinion, declared that neither slaves nor free blacks could ever be citizens with legal rights, that slaves were property, and that property, whether inanimate or animate, could be moved from one state or territory to another without ceasing to be property.

Chief Justice Roger Taney wrote the majority decision in *Dred Scott v. Sandford*. A furious Abraham Lincoln urged fellow Republicans to refuse to obey it. *Courtesy of the Library of Congress.*

The decision infuriated slavery's opponents. Abraham Lincoln, for one, insisted that he and his Republican colleagues should "refuse to obey it as a political rule."[46] To add fuel to the fire, it soon became public knowledge that Buchanan had meddled with the Court, even though in his inaugural address he pretended that he didn't know the decision had already been made by announcing that he would "cheerfully submit" to whatever ruling the Court handed down. Buchanan's involvement in this unhappy affair, which further divided the nation and brought charges of hypocrisy or worse to his door, was so uncharacteristically heavy-handed that it's reasonable to suppose illness clouded his judgment.

A similar clumsiness was obvious in Buchanan's inaugural address. In terms of raw numbers, Buchanan had bested Republican opponent John C. Frémont by only 500,000 votes, transforming the Republican loss, as one of Frémont's supporters put it, into a "victorious defeat." Although Buchanan had won, he surely must have seen that the final tally was a graphic warning of the deep and dangerously heated divide in the nation over slavery. As president-elect, the prudent thing to do would have been to write an inaugural address intended to still the troubled waters. Instead, just as Pierce had done in his final message to Congress, Buchanan made it more than clear that he sided with the proslavery faction by brushing aside Republican objections to the spread of slavery into the territories. In fact, he declared that the "long agitation" stirred up by antislavery extremists both failed to improve the conditions of slaves and "alienated and estranged the people of the sister States from each other." Therefore, he urged his fellow citizens, "Let every Union-loving man exert his best influence to suppress this agitation."[47] Buchanan's remarks, doubtlessly delivered with clench-jawed intensity given the fact that his physical distress barely allowed him to stand at the inaugural podium, were needlessly impolitic and out of character for a temperamentally cautious man. Once again, it's possible that they were born of the irritability and impatience that comes from sickness. The symptoms associated with the National Hotel disease had returned with a vengeance as he struggled in Wheatland to finish writing his speech, and some of the stress and misery they brought him found their way into the tone of his text. Given the volatility of the times, it was a most unfortunate tone.

It would be going too far to suppose that the psychological and physical debility inflicted on Buchanan by the National Hotel disease somehow changed his basic political outlook. Like his predecessor Franklin Pierce, Buchanan was a doughface who hated Republicans and sympathized with the South when it came to the slavery issue. Most of the cabinet members he appointed were southerners, and the cronies with whom he drank were largely from the South. What was new in the first weeks of his administration was the sharp edge with which he publicly defended these beliefs. It wasn't his convictions that had changed but the native caution that had made him the play-it-safe bureaucrat throughout all his years of public service. Old Public Functionary, irritable and unsteady from the illness gnawing at his bowels, was out of character.

A Bad Start

As will be seen in the next chapter, the National Hotel disease frightened the citizens of Washington and a good segment of the American public in general. The suddenness of the disease, its unknown origin and its debilitating and long-lasting symptoms created a near panic for a few weeks.

Through it all, Buchanan and his handlers tried to reassure the American people that all was well with the president, despite the persistently circulating rumors that he was at death's door. Even though not coming close to dying at the hands of the mysterious illness, Buchanan was incapacitated enough to stumble in two important ways at the beginning of his term. In less troubled times, temporary fogginess of judgment, irritability of temper and general malaise in a chief executive might have done little harm. But in 1857, in a nation sitting on a powder keg of partisan wrangling, sectional discord and outright fighting in the Kansas territory, it was yet another spark that eventually helped light the fuse of war. The administration, which would have been distrusted by half of the country in the best of times, got off to an especially bad start. One of the causes of that was the National Hotel disease.

IV

A NATIONAL PANIC

The opinion is becoming very general that the sickness at the National Hotel in Washington, which commenced about the date of the inauguration of President Buchanan, was the result of a deliberate and fiendish attempt to poison the President and his nearest friends!
—Pittsfield Sun, *May 7, 1857*

On the last day of March 1857, the *Lancaster Evening Express*, one of the dailies in President Buchanan's hometown, reported the death of Mr. Elliot Eskridge Lane. Only thirty-three years old, he had succumbed to what the *Express* called an "inflammation of the stomach, tending to gangrene." The young man had been "indisposed" since staying at the National Hotel during the presidential inauguration. His death notice went on to note that "although not confined to his room," Lane "had been suffering slightly with the symptoms which have marked all the cases of disease contracted at the National." When he took a sudden turn for the worse, one of Lancaster's leading physicians was summoned, but he "saw at once that his patient was beyond the reach of medical skill."

Mid-nineteenth-century journalism had its own kind of wire service: editors simply lifted stories whole cloth from other newspapers, sometimes with attribution, often without. It wasn't long before Lane's death notice appeared in papers whose circulations were hundreds of miles from Lancaster. The young man who had been unknown in life suddenly became a celebrity in death, first because he was President Buchanan's nephew and brother to

Harriet Lane, the niece who served as bachelor James Buchanan's Executive Mansion hostess, was sister to one of the first recorded victims of the National Hotel disease. A Pennsylvania newspaper announced that the death of Elliot Eskridge Lane was caused by poison, helping to launch months of panic. *Courtesy of the Library of Congress.*

Harriet Lane, the young woman who served as her bachelor uncle's hostess in the Executive Mansion, second because he had been Buchanan's personal secretary and third because his fatal illness was associated with the National Hotel. His death was the first noteworthy one to be linked to the mysterious sickness that laid Buchanan and others low.

It didn't much matter that just the day before the *Evening Express* insinuated a connection between Lane's death and the National Hotel, its rival, the *Lancaster Inland Daily*, more soberly announced that the youth had died of "inflammation of the bowels resulting from a cold caught while planting trees at Wheatland." The public was primed by three weeks' worth of rumors and innuendoes, some of them in print but many circulating by word of mouth, about the illness at the National Hotel. People then as now were intrigued by newspaper accounts of mysterious deaths, and it was much more exciting to believe that young Lane was the first victim of something ominously inscrutable than to attribute his death to a humdrum "inflammation of the bowels resulting from a cold."

During the months following Lane's death, right up through the summer and even into the following year, newspapers and journals were full of speculations about the cause of the National Hotel disease, alarming death notices of its alleged victims, and firsthand accounts of patients who suffered from it. Residents of New York City, Chicago, Philadelphia, Boston, Baltimore and small towns in between followed the latest news with keen interest. But the citizens of Washington, at least during the first few weeks of the public buzz, were panicked. They were, after all, in close proximity to the affliction's point of origin, and so had a very personal stake in it. For all they knew, the malady wasn't confined to the National Hotel, but was waiting to erupt in other parts of the city as well. As it gradually became clear that the illness seemed peculiar to the National, the immediate panic began to give way—but not before the National was forced to close its doors for a time because people were too frightened to eat or lodge in it.

Two main theories about the affliction's cause were debated in the newspapers and medical journals, not to mention saloons, drawing rooms and even the President's House. One was that the victims had been poisoned; this view was especially bandied about in the popular press. The other was that they had been felled by dangerously putrid vapors arising from backed-up sewers; this was the considered opinion of the medical authorities and scientists who examined the case. By the time the National Hotel disease scare more or less died down in July 1857, the vapors hypothesis had won general acceptance. But suspicions of poison lingered on in many quarters and would resurface years afterwards.

OUTBREAK IN WASHINGTON, D.C.

THE POISON HYPOTHESIS

Given the acrimonious political climate, as well as the fact that president-elect Buchanan and several of his cronies were stricken, it was only natural that some would suspect the National Hotel disease was actually a dastardly attempt to poison the Democrat from Pennsylvania and put an end to his administration before it could get under way. The *Baltimore Sun* was one of the first newspapers to suggest a plot to kill Buchanan. On April 1, 1857, it ran this chilling notice: "A *post mortem* examination of the remains of a gentleman who died in Pennsylvania from disease contracted at the National Hotel shows a deposit of arsenic in the stomach. A patient here now suffers an enlargement of the abdomen from some cause, and with marked symptoms of being poisoned." It's not at all clear who the Pennsylvania gentleman was. Quite possibly, he was Elliot Eskridge Lane, but there's no evidence to suggest that Lane's corpse was autopsied. So the "deposit of arsenic in the stomach" is most likely purple speculation. Likewise, the patient in Baltimore suffering from "an enlargement of the abdomen" remains anonymous. Was his illness connected with the National Hotel in any way? Why was a distention of the belly immediately assumed to be a symptom of poisoning rather than some natural malady? The *Baltimore Sun*'s short piece, picked up by the *New York Daily Times* three days later and subsequently reprinted in a number of other papers, was entirely absent of any substantiation. But it set in motion frightened whispers of sinister conspirators.

Less than a month after young Lane's death, another dignitary who had lodged at the National Hotel during Buchanan's inauguration died. His symptoms, like Lane's, were intestinal: violent diarrhea, frothy stool, vomiting, extreme thirst from dehydration and lassitude. The victim this time was no less than a United States representative, John G. Montgomery from Pennsylvania's Thirty-Fifth District. One of Buchanan's fellow Democrats, Montgomery had taken his seat in Congress less than two months before his death. Immediately following the inauguration, too ill to perform his duties, he returned to his home in Danville, a small town in central Pennsylvania, where he languished and died. On April 27, 1857, three days after Montgomery's death, the *Pennsylvanian* announced his demise in terms that left no doubt as to the cause of death. "Every feature in his disease," the obituary ran, "indicated the presence of arsenic in his system."

Like the *Baltimore Sun*'s accusation of poison a month earlier, this one was likewise widely reprinted. The *New York Daily Herald* picked up the story three days later, and by May 9, it had traveled westward far enough to be paraphrased and elaborated upon in the *Weekly Wisconsin Patriot*. Under the headline "Attempt to Poison the President," the *Patriot* reported that "there were certain coincidences" in Montgomery's death "suggestive of the most horrible suspicions. Mr. Buchanan arrived at the Hotel on the 25th [*sic*] of January, and on the next day the first case of this disease occurred; and in a few days there were about forty cases." After Buchanan returned to Wheatland, the article continued, there were no new cases of the disease until he and his party returned in early March for the inauguration. "Then the disease broke out with increased violence, and many hundreds were affected. The symptoms uniformly indicated poison." The death notices of Montgomery that traveled across the nation somehow made more plausible the possibility that the National Hotel disease was actually a crime. A statesman had fallen, and this time there had to be a deeper reason than a mere inflammation of the bowels.

But, of course, three necessary conditions for any crime are the presence of a criminal, a motive for committing the crime in the first place and an opportunity. If the illnesses of Buchanan, Lane, Montgomery and from forty to seven hundred others (the numbers of the afflicted cited by the press swung wildly) who stayed at the National Hotel were due to poison, who was responsible, why and how?

In both the press and popular imagination, there was no shortage of suspects. Some opined that the radical abolitionists—frequently and inaccurately identified with Black Republicans—had attempted to assassinate the doughface Buchanan because of his soft stand on slavery. The *Brooklyn Eagle*, a Democratic paper, proclaimed on May 7 that the same antislavery zealots it blamed for stirring up trouble in the Kansas territory were perfectly capable of poisoning a proslavery president.

> *Poisoning was the work of the same reckless, bloodthirsty spirit that armed hords* [sic] *of brigands to go forth and slay and murder in Kansas. The spirit of murder and violence had been invoked by a portion of the more fanatical supporters of Fremont during the Presidential campaign; and if crazy zealots, whose rifles had been consecrated to the work of assassination in a distant Territory, should fail to see any moral distinction between the application of lead to an advocate of a Presidential candidate, and arsenic to himself, it is more to be regretted than marveled at.*

Proslavery newspapers repeated accusations like this with gusto. But many readers, even those who despised the Black Republicans and abolitionists,

Kentucky-born John C. Breckinridge, Buchanan's vice president, was an even more ardent supporter of slavery's expansion than the president. Nevertheless, some believed that abolitionists had poisoned Buchanan to clear the way for a Breckinridge presidency. *Courtesy of the Library of Congress.*

found them less than credible. Buchanan's vice president, John C. Breckinridge, was a Kentuckian who supported the peculiar institution with an ardor never displayed by Buchanan. When southern states began seceding from the Union in late 1860, in fact, Breckinridge threw his hat in with the Confederacy and served as one of its generals during the Civil War. The claim that opponents of slavery tried to poison Buchanan because of his proslavery position thus made little tactical sense. What would be the logic of assassinating a doughface president only to have a Southerner succeed him?

Another rumor making the rounds was that Southern secessionists were behind the plot to poison the president-elect. Their alleged motive wasn't so much to get Breckinridge in the White House as to create a countrywide scandal that would accelerate a split between the North and the South. Given the vitriolic hatred of the North felt by secessionist "fire-eaters," as they were called, it's not unimaginable that at least some of them would have been glad to see such a plot carried out. But since both Buchanan and Breckinridge were friends and protectors of slaveholders, assassinating the president-elect of the United States to further the interests of slaveholders seemed pointless.

Pointing the finger at abolitionists appealed to pro-slavers, and targeting fire-eaters was popular with opponents of slavery. But there was a third set of possible suspects that some members of both camps denounced: blacks. The *Cincinnati Commercial*, a paper that had supported Frémont during the presidential election, suggested this possibility on May 7. "The negroes," it argued, "had been moved to this crime by the language of Democrats."

They were taught by the pro-slavery political brawlers that if Frémont was elected the niggers would be free, and not only that, but the rulers of the country; while, if Mr. Buchanan should be President, the question against them would be settled forever. The poor negroes, interested by this slang, and but dimly conscious of the character and necessary incidents of the struggle actually going on, and by nature inclined to personal principles, became impressed that Frémont was their friend and Buchanan their enemy, and it is not improbable that they knew no more of the nature of the election than to suppose that if Buchanan were out of the way Frémont must be President and themselves free.

In Washington, a version of this theory that became popular for a time was that disgruntled black servants at the National Hotel had poisoned the food or drink, or both, of Buchanan and his Democrat circle to punish them for their support of slavery. Racial distrust and dislike of blacks was deeply embedded in both the North and the South, and even those whites who opposed the spread of slavery outside the southern states generally neither liked blacks nor welcomed them into their communities. (Witness, for example, the patronizing language of the earlier quoted *Cincinnati Commercial* piece.) So it was easy for many whites to believe that disgruntled blacks may have been behind the National Hotel outbreak. Moreover, speculation ran, as servants in the hotel they certainly had opportunity. The only problem with this theory, as things turned out, was that the current proprietors of the National Hotel didn't employ blacks, either free or enslaved. The cooks, waiters and cleaners were all white, mainly Irish immigrants, who had no obvious reason to want to do harm to Buchanan and the Democrats. In fact, most Irish, traditionally courted by the Democrat Party, voted for Buchanan.[48]

So much for the suspects. What about opportunity? If there was a deliberate poisoning of Buchanan and his friends—a poisoning, moreover, that somehow got out of hand and sickened dozens more than the perpetrators intended—how was it pulled off?

The difficulty in ascertaining the means of poisoning was that even though some guests at the National Hotel sickened, not all of them did. To explain this, some conspiracy theorists pointed out that Buchanan and his cronies were tea drinkers who drank their beverage the Southern way, with lots of sugar. So they concluded that arsenic must have been surreptitiously mixed into sugar bowls, which targeted Buchanan and company but also, unfortunately, smote other guests as well. That the conspirators willingly inflicted collateral damage was yet one more indication, newspapers blared, of their wickedness.

Another theory had it that the poisoning was done secondhand. After city officials inspected the National in the wake of the outbreak, they allegedly discovered several drowned rats in the hotel's water tank. Suspicions flew that the rats had been poisoned with arsenic and then deliberately thrown into the cistern to decompose and poison the water as well. But this theory was far-fetched, not the least because it failed to explain why only some of the water-drinking guests fell ill. It also stretched credulity to imagine that the tiny amount of arsenic sufficient to poison a rat would be sufficient to render an entire tank of water toxic.

Eventually, the theory that Buchanan had been criminally poisoned fell out of favor, although a few holdouts stubbornly clung to it. One of them was the editor of the *Maine Farmer*, who on April 30, 1857, insisted, by that point quite inaccurately, that it was "the opinion of many persons that there was a deliberate purpose to poison Mr. Buchanan; and that the diabolical scoundrel hazarded the lives of thousands in the attempt." On May 7, the Washington-based *National Era* blasted a report from the city's board of health that denied the possibility of deliberate poisoning. The official investigation into the National Hotel disease, the paper charged, was conducted too late, after the outbreak had already run its course. Consequently, the conclusions summarized in the report were suspect, and the *Era* hinted darkly at the likelihood of an assassination attempt. But just a day later, on May 8, the *New York Daily Times* published a comment by one G.P. Buell that seemed to crystalize the absurdity of all the deliberate poisoning rumors. Buell said that soon after the hotel guests were stricken, he interviewed a man who had been a head steward there. The man spoke in sharp terms about the hotel, at which he was no longer employed, calling the "d—d place" "nothing but a hospital, which no one could remain in it with safety." But then the truth came out. "He then indulged in a perfect torrent of abuse of the proprietors; his invective was personal and continual," convincing Buell that the ex-steward's accusations "were prompted by no motive short of the gratification of personal revenge."

Conspiracy theories about a failed assassination attempt having lost credibility except to those who refused to weigh the evidence, attention shifted to the possibility of accidental arsenic poisoning. Two competing theories emerged.

One had to do with the rats supposedly discovered in the hotel's water tank. Perhaps they had ingested arsenic innocently placed in the hotel's nooks and crannies for the purpose of killing them off. The poison had caused them to become desperately thirsty, and they had plunged into the National's tank to assuage their thirst and subsequently drowned. As their bodies decomposed, the arsenic in their systems polluted the hotel's drinking water. On the surface, this explanation seemed credible. In fact, of all the rumors circulating about the cause of the National Hotel disease, this one was the flimsiest. First, the mystery of why only a few people fell ill remained unsolved. Additionally, it's not clear that a rat that had eaten arsenic would have had enough energy or even life to make it to the hotel's cistern. Finally, the same objection to the theory that deliberately poisoned rats had been thrown into the cistern applied to this one: the minute amount of arsenic in a rat's corpse would harmlessly dilute in an entire tank of water.

The other theory of accidental poisoning, vigorously proposed by a Scottish-born chemist who had immigrated to the United States, suggested that the guests who fell ill were, true enough, suffering from arsenic poisoning. But it was the result of copper saucepans and pots whose protective coating of tin had worn thin, thus allowing the copper, which contained arsenic, to taint the victuals cooked in them. This seemed a possibility worth taking seriously until two discoveries came to light. The first was that city inspectors who carefully examined the hotel's cookware found no evidence that pots had shed their tin coating. The second discovery was that some people who had slept in the hotel but had neither supped nor drank there also fell ill. This all but put an end to the likelihood that Buchanan had been poisoned accidentally, and the proprietors of the hotel, who insisted that the "unfortunate affair has worked our ruin," published an open letter in the March 27, 1857 edition of the *Boston Daily* to that effect. "It has been a current report," they wrote, "that the sickness was caused by poisoned rats getting into the water tanks. This story is a lie, without foundation. We do not believe it possible that any poison could have been put into the food, as we know that persons have been attacked by the disease, who have frequented the house, and never tasted food in it." The letter was, of course, a self-serving attempt of the owners to deny liability for the sickness that originated in their establishment. But their denial also just happened to be true. Neither the accidental nor deliberate poisoning of food or drink seemed a likely explanation.

The suspicion that Buchanan and the other guests had been poisoned was contradicted, finally, by the victims' symptoms. Several physicians came forward to announce that, in their judgment, a diagnosis of "mineral poisoning" simply didn't fit the illness. Arsenic would have had an immediate effect on those who ingested it. Nearly all the victims of the mysterious hotel

Although one of the most posh hotels on Pennsylvania Avenue, the National Hotel's reputation was damaged nearly beyond repair by the illness that erupted in it. It eventually had to close down until the panic subsided. *Courtesy of the Library of Congress.*

disease displayed symptoms only gradually and, afterward, intermittently. Severe stomach cramping would have likely accompanied arsenic poisoning. The victims experienced bloating, nausea and diarrhea but very little cramping. Finally, the one and only documented autopsy performed on a victim of the illness revealed no evidence of arsenic poisoning. Major George McNeir, a man of sixty-four years, had fallen ill on January 9, 1857, long before Buchanan's first visit, almost immediately after eating at the National Hotel. He was atypical in falling ill so quickly, but his symptoms were in keeping with the ones associated with the outbreak. For the next five months, he suffered intermittently, finally dying in July. The autopsy revealed that the cause of McNeir's death was a "catarrhal inflammation of the mucous membrane of the large intestine," a conclusion that accorded with the description of what had killed young Elliot Lane, President Buchanan's nephew, several months earlier. The scientific conclusion was that arsenic couldn't have caused such a condition.[49]

THE MIASMA HYPOTHESIS

An alternative explanation for the sickness that befell National Hotel guests focused on "miasma," a now-archaic word for unhealthy or "mephitic" vapors. In the first half of the nineteenth century, prior to the emergence of germ theory, two explanations of the origin of diseases competed with one another. The contagion hypothesis held that illnesses such as cholera, plague, typhus and yellow fever that infected large communities of people were transmitted through actual physical touch. Sick persons infected healthy ones by direct contact. The miasma hypothesis, on the other hand, argued that illnesses were generated and spread by gases or vapors arising from putrid matter. ("Miasma" is derived from a Greek word meaning "pollution.") Proponents of this theory, arguing that it was unlikely that widespread contagions could spread simply by physical contact, contended that "damp earth, stagnant water and putrefied or decayed animal and vegetable matter released noxious and toxic fumes, which in turn contaminated the atmosphere and produced disease."[50] The popularity of this explanation accounted for why cities of the period tended to build open, street-level sewers rather than underground drain systems. The rationale was that organic matter such as human waste, garbage and animal corpses, if allowed to decay quickly in the open air and sunlight, would pose less of a disease threat than if clogged in pipes. Stewing in wetness and filth, the putrefaction process for such trapped refuse would last longer and produce more deadly miasma.

In early March, Washington's mayor ordered the city's board of health to look into the National Hotel mystery. A subcommittee of investigators was organized and several inspectors were dispatched to examine the building. By then, rumors of poisoning were being thrown about with abandon in both newspapers and street gossip, and the subcommittee took some pains to scrutinize their likelihood. When the official report was released toward the end of the month—a report, it will be recalled, subsequently blasted by the *National Era*—it firmly rejected poison as a viable cause of the affliction, plunking down instead for miasma. It defended its conclusion on the basis of six observations. There was no sign of filth or rotting organic material in the National Hotel. Everything was "well kept in all its departments." Likewise, the stored food in the kitchen and pantry was "in healthy condition," and no lard, which might have gone bad and caused the symptoms suffered by guests, had been used in the hotel since before Christmas the year before. The subcommittee decided that it was impossible that rats could have somehow squeezed into the hotel's water tanks, thus dismissing the indirect poisoning hypothesis. But most telling were the subcommittee report's final two points. Investigators found that several guests who had lodged but not eaten in the hotel also fell ill, and that others who had eaten but who had kept their room windows open didn't get sick. The conclusion was that the source of the illness must have been in the air, not the food or drink.[51]

So, what had happened? How did the foul air infiltrate the National Hotel to begin with? At least one commentator, Dr. David Boswell Reid, the Scottish chemist who originally defended the theory that arsenic poison from de-tinned copper pots and pans might be the culprit, opined that the poisonous miasma was from arsenic. He adopted this position after it was pointed out to him that people who hadn't supped at the hotel also fell ill with the mysterious malady. Reluctant to let the arsenic poisoning hypothesis go, he speculated on May 1 in the *American Publishers' Circular and Literary Gazette* on a different cause for it: atmospheric rather than food dispersal. It was a wild suggestion, since it wasn't at all clear how poisonous vapors could arise from cooking utensils. But Reid's voice was one that couldn't be easily ignored. He was a pioneer in the movement to provide adequate ventilation to city dwellings, in particular crowded tenement buildings. Later in the same year that the National Hotel disease alarmed the nation, Reid published a groundbreaking book, *Ventilation in American Dwellings*, in which he pled for better air flow in large hotels in order to avoid similar outbreaks in the future. As an illustration of the dangers of badly ventilated public houses, he referenced the "noted case of the National Hotel at Washington, where so many hundreds suffered very lately." By the time the book appeared, Reid was no longer confident that the source of the illness was traceable to atmospheric arsenic. But testimony from several persons "gave proof that there was, in one part of the hotel at least, a discharge of vitiated air from drains of so intense a character that it produced instantaneous vomiting on some occasions and affected numbers in a less degree at the moment, who were nevertheless attacked at a subsequent period."[52]

Reid was accurate in his report that several people who had lodged at the National had noticed a noxious aroma around the time of the outbreak. One of them, an anonymous letter-writer to the *New York Daily Times*, reported on May 13 that he and several fellow guests had taken ill as early as mid-December. He and his wife, he reported, had both noticed a foul odor in their room, which just happened to be the same one that president-elect Buchanan lodged in a few weeks later. In the May 2 edition of the *Lowell Daily Citizen*, the eminent Dr. Charles T. Jackson reported that he was treating a patient who had fallen ill after being affected by a disagreeable aroma experienced in the National. Because his patient hadn't dined at the hotel, Jackson, like many others, concluded that it was "very easy to prove" that the source of the illness must have been airborne.

Reports of disgusting odors in the National both clinched the miasma theory in the minds of most of the day's scientists and pretty much ruled out Reid's initial arsenic hypothesis. After all, airborne arsenic wouldn't smell like rotting offal. The general suspicion then focused on sewage lines leading to and from the hotel as the culprits. Even then, there was disagreement about what had happened. Winter in Washington during 1856–57 had been particularly brutal, and this led some to speculate that aboveground sewage drains leading from establishments and homes had frozen, backed up and pushed toxic fumes indoors, which normally would have dispersed harmlessly into the open air. It was noted that the worst of the outbreaks, both the one in late January that afflicted Buchanan and the one that recurred in the week before his inauguration, struck during two horrible cold snaps. The combination of frozen drains and closed windows, this account concluded, led to a poisonous atmosphere in the hotel, especially in those rooms, such as Buchanan's, situated directly above the drains.

Others suggested a quite different cause for the sewage backup. In early January, the cold weather had given way briefly to a warm period of rain and snowmelt, which caused the Potomac River to rise. Again, in March, the cold was relieved by a warm spell on inauguration day, leading once again to a sudden melt-off of ice and snow. This led Isaac O. Barnes, himself a victim of the first outbreak, to suggest that the "noxious vapor" that had invaded the National "was driven back upon and into the cellar by the sudden rise of the Potomac, into which the sewer should empty itself."[53] To his mind, the poisoning was due to warm, not cold, weather.

There was even a third explanation for the backup. *Scientific American* reported at the end of March that the odor in the National that afflicted the guests with nausea and diarrhea was caused by the tapping of sewers at Sixth and Pennsylvania Avenues.[54] Critics were quick to point out that other establishments in the vicinity that used the same sewer lines hadn't been similarly affected. But this same argument could be applied to the frozen sewers and flooded sewers hypotheses as well—a conclusion that, in the minds of some, reopened the door to the poisoned food theory.

Regardless of the continuing perplexity over the source or sources of the toxic miasma, by summer, the scientific community was for the most part satisfied that the National Hotel disease was an airborne infection. The subcommittee appointed by the Washington Board of Health to investigate the outbreak eventually went with this conclusion, prompting the District's mayor to chide the National's owners for not providing better ventilation in their establishment. The owners, in turn, despite their insistence that they were blameless in the matter, closed the hotel for a while and even sold off its furniture, apparently worried that beds and chairs might have absorbed toxins from the foul air. *Scientific American*, one of the leading scientific journals in the nation, concluded that the symptoms most likely indicated a form of "light cholera" disseminated by the hotel's noxious atmosphere.[55] The New York Academy of Medicine likewise endorsed the miasma theory because its experts concluded that the only common denominator that tied all the cases together was foul air. The *Ohio Medical and Surgical Journal* announced that fumes arising from "imperfect sewage" were the most likely cause of the symptoms endured by the National's guests.[56]

Doubts continued to linger in the general population, which showed itself reluctant to let go of the thrilling possibility that the National Hotel disease was a botched attempt to assassinate Buchanan. But a public hungry for gossip has a short attention span, and excited talk about arsenic poisoning, murderous blacks, rascally Republicans and conspiratorial fire-eaters eventually fizzled out. As one columnist wrote in May, "I cannot but believe" that the "speculations, theories and conjectures usque ad nauseam" about "this literally sickening subject" have wearied everyone.[57]

THE FINAL VERDICT

Even though the miasma theory of illness was false and in fact would be supplanted within a generation by the germ theory, the scientists, physicians and chemists who pronounced foul air the cause of the National Hotel disease came admirably close to an accurate explanation of the outbreak. They recognized that the symptoms suffered by the victims didn't fit the profile of mineral poisoning, a conclusion verified to some extent by the autopsy of Major McNeir. They correctly concluded that the backup of sewage in the National had something to do with the cause of the disease. They were, of course, wrong about how the sewage actually caused the illness, believing as they did that the stench itself was unhealthy and disease-laden, such that merely to breathe it in was to somehow ingest the toxin that inflicted victims with intermittent nausea, diarrhea, dehydration and sometimes death.

What they couldn't know before the groundbreaking research of Louis Pasteur and Robert Koch later on in the century was that the source of the illness was a microscopic particle that would come to be called "germ" or "bacterium."

Scientific American was almost certainly correct when it diagnosed the National Hotel disease as cholera. Regardless of how the hotel's sewer lines backed up—whether they froze or were prevented from draining into the Potomac because of an unexpected mid-winter thaw—the likely scenario is that raw sewage somehow leaked into the National's kitchens where cooks and waiters, nearly all of whom fell ill with the malady themselves, came into physical contact with it. Perhaps the sewage somehow leaked into and polluted the hotel's drinking and cooking water. Maybe in cleaning up backed-up sewage spills, a kitchen worker accidentally transmitted the bacteria to utensils or cutlery that then infected guests. One thing is certain: the illness was communicated by food and drink, not by noxious vapors. The stench noted by many of the guests was a signal that illness might be lurking but wasn't the illness itself.

The miasma theory of transmission gave way in the late nineteenth century to the germ theory championed by Louis Pasteur. *Courtesy of the Library of Congress.*

Robert Koch's discovery of the tuberculosis, cholera and anthrax bacilli laid the miasma theory to rest once and for all. *Courtesy of the Library of Congress.*

79

It's not clear why some patrons who ate and drank at the National escaped infection. Perhaps their constitutions were especially strong, or perhaps they were simply lucky. It's also not clear what to make of newspaper claims that some people who merely lodged at the hotel also fell ill, stories that convinced many that the disease had to be airborne. Either the reports were mistaken—that is, that everyone who displayed symptoms *did* eat at the hotel—or the cholera infection wasn't confined to the National. But given that there were so few reports of non-National patrons falling ill, the first possibility is the stronger one, even though why a disease so infectious that it was commonly called "King Cholera" remained so isolated is perplexing. It was precisely such puzzles that lent credence, some years later, to a revival of the conspiratorial poisoning theory.

V

THE ALLURE OF CONSPIRACY

There is a style of mind that…I call…the paranoid style simply because no other word adequately evokes the sense of heated exaggeration, suspiciousness, and conspiratorial fantasy that I have in mind.
—Richard Hofstadter[58]

Despite the lack of evidence, rumors that Buchanan's illness was caused by a botched assassination attempt continued right up into the twentieth century. As late as 1933, the *Washington Post* for March 4 endorsed such a theory in a long article, published under the screaming banner "BUCHANAN ESCAPED TWO ASSASSINATION PLOTS," that was chock full of factual misstatements. The *Post* may have been the most reputable trumpeter of the claim that there had been a plot afoot to murder Buchanan, but it was by no means the only one. No fewer than three accounts, wildly differing from one another in their speculations, made the rounds in the years following the initial panic caused by the National Hotel disease. One revived the argument that Southern defenders of slavery had plotted the attempt on Buchanan's life. Another resurrected the claim that it was abolitionists, not slave owners, who wanted the president-elect dead. And in the early twentieth century, a potboiler appeared that insisted Buchanan had been nearly done in by an ominous Roman Catholic plot.

THE PARANOID STYLE

A generation ago, noted historian Richard Hofstadter published an influential essay in which he argued that a detectable strain of paranoia runs through American politics. He didn't intend to use the word in a straightforwardly clinical sense, but rather, as he said, to suggest a tendency to engage in hyperbole, suspicion and "conspiratorial fantasy." This tendency, argued Hofstadter, was exemplified in the anti-masonry rhetoric of the eighteenth century, the anti-Catholicism of the nineteenth and the anti-communism of Joe McCarthy and his House Un-American Activities Committee of the twentieth.

What characterizes these and other eruptions of paranoia in American politics is their insistence on seeing the world in stark black-and-white terms when it comes to morality and truth. The paranoiac lacks a sense of subtlety or an appreciation of ambiguity. For him, there is simply good and evil, truth and falsehood, with no middle ground whatsoever. Moreover, evil and falsehood lurk everywhere, conspiring to wreck their havoc on virtue and truth at every available opportunity. Evil forces, enslaved by their own greed and lust for power, diabolically and tirelessly work behind the scenes to control the nation, thus requiring the champions of virtue and truth to be ever vigilant. Needless to say, such a worldview encourages its holders to demonize anyone they consider to be a threat. As Hofstadter put it:

> *The enemy is clearly delineated* [by the paranoiac]: *he is a perfect model of malice, a kind of amoral superman—sinister, ubiquitous, powerful, cruel, sensual, luxury-loving. Unlike the rest of us, the enemy is not caught in the toils of the vast mechanism of history, himself a victim of his past, his desires, his limitations. He wills, indeed he manufactures, the mechanism of history, or tries to deflect the normal course of history in an evil way. He makes crises, starts runs on banks, causes depressions, manufactures disasters and then enjoys and profits from the misery he has produced. The paranoid's interpretation of history is distinctly personal: decisive events are not taken as part of the stream of history, but as the consequences of someone's will. Very often the enemy is held to possess some especially effective source of power: he controls the press; he has unlimited funds; he has a new secret for influencing the mind (brainwashing); he has a special technique for seduction (the Catholic confessional).*[59]

This may seem a chilling way of viewing the world, and there's no doubt that at one level Hofstadter's paranoiacs live anxious existences. But they also derive a perverse kind of comfort from imagining a conspiracy around every corner because doing so imposes a pattern of meaning upon a world that otherwise might seem frighteningly unpredictable at times. Sometimes, unforeseeable bad things happen for unexciting, pedestrian reasons: a disgruntled loser shoots a president during a 1963 motorcade through Dallas. That the course of history can be changed by such a random event is too much for a paranoiac to handle, so he immediately begins looking for a vast and complex conspiracy that will restore an orderly pattern to his world. In the paranoiac's mind, then, President Kennedy had to have been killed by rogue CIA agents, or a threatened Mafia, or a vengeful Fidel Castro, or even his own vice president. To the non-paranoiac observer, the very byzantine complexity of such conspiracy theories makes them suspicious. But to the paranoiac, they are the bizarre guarantees of a systematic, and hence ultimately non-chaotic, world. And since there are so many seemingly random events that call order into question, the paranoiac conspiracy buff generally thinks of the world as a vast network of behind-the-scenes machinations. He's likely to be a champion of more than one conspiracy, convinced as he is that there are many powerbrokers secretly pulling strings to bend society to their will.

The conspiracy theories about the "real" nature of the National Hotel disease examined here display all of these paranoid characteristics. Each of them posits the existence of an enemy wicked enough to stop at nothing. Each of them apparently needs to believe that Buchanan's illness was more deeply meaningful than the consequence of an accidental back-up of sewage. And all three of them posit multiple conspiracies to murder presidents, with Buchanan being just one of several actual or intended victims.

THE SLAVE POWER CONSPIRACY

In 1853, Edinburgh-based *Blackwood's Magazine*, one of the most popular journals of its day, published an exposé of what was popularly known as the Slave Power, a supposed cabal of Southern powerbrokers intent on controlling all branches of the federal government in order to spread slavery throughout the entire United States. *Blackwood's* alleged that the Slave Power exercised "control in and over the United States...more absolute than that of any European aristocracy—almost as uncontrolled by public sentiment as an Asiatic potentate."[60]

This was hyperbole taken to its ultimate level. But it voiced a deep-seated suspicion, held by many Northerners, that Southern ambitions warranted close watch. Ex-president and congressman John Quincy Adams, Massachusetts senator Charles Sumner, Harvard president Josiah Quincy and *New York Tribune* editor Horace Greeley were just a few of the Northern luminaries who accepted the existence of a Southern strategy to dominate the government. Abraham Lincoln not only believed in it but also publicly accused Stephen Douglas of being part of it when the two men vied for the same Senate seat in 1858.

Nor could it be denied that there was some reason to take Slave Power worries seriously. Although the North had a larger white population than the South and was certainly more developed industrially, southern-born men seemed to be in near-perpetual control of the government from the Republic's very birth. Southerners served as the nation's chief executives for forty-nine of the seventy-two years between the presidencies of Washington and Lincoln. In eleven more of those years, three northern-born presidents—Millard Fillmore, Franklin Pierce and James Buchanan—were markedly sympathetic to the South. Between 1789 and 1861, twenty out of thirty-five Supreme Court justices were Southerners, constituting a majority on the Court at any given time. Twenty-three of thirty-six Speakers of the House were from the South, and so were twenty-four of thirty-six presidents pro tem of the Senate.

Moreover, in the years immediately leading up to the Civil War, many in the North believed that the South was holding the nation hostage by repeatedly threatening secession in order to wrest concessions to slavery. Most of the threats were sheer bluff. But so-called fire-eating Southerners who actually did want to form a separate, slave-holding nation relentlessly bullied politicians, Northern as well as Southern ones, and arrogantly proclaimed the superiority of Southern to Northern culture. (One of them, Mississippi's John Quitman, who marched in Buchanan's inaugural parade, succumbed to the National Hotel disease.) South Carolina's James Hammond spoke for them when he crowed in his 1858 "Cotton Is King" speech that the South was invincible because it produced the world's cotton and that Northern banks and business was irremediably beholden to it. His message was clear: the North would be wise to bend to the South.

Given the popularity of the belief that there indeed was a Slave Power conspiracy to control the government, it's not surprising that many Northerners concluded that when the Southern states finally did secede it was just part of the Slave Power's nefarious plan to carve out a vast slave

Contrary to rumors that only Northerners died from the National Hotel "poisoning," one of the victims was influential Mississippi statesman John Quitman. *Courtesy of the Library of Congress.*

empire stretching from coast to coast as well as southward to include Cuba and Nicaragua. In 1864, one John Smith Dye published a potboiler arguing for precisely this thesis. His book, *The Adder's Den; or, Secrets of the Great Conspiracy to Overthrow Liberty in America,* was a heated indictment of Southern ambition. Even more, Dye alleged that Slave Power agents had conspired to murder any and all presidents who stood in the way of Southern expansion. According to Dye, the Slave Power had made attempts on the lives of four presidents, including James Buchanan, and had actually succeeded in murdering two of them. His book caused a sensation when it first appeared. But when it was reissued two years later on the heels of Abraham Lincoln's assassination, many readers far and wide, reeling from the murder of the

In his potboiler *The Adder's Den*, John Smith Dye argued that the Slave Power failed at an attempt on President Andrew Jackson's life. Jackson is pictured above. *Courtesy of the Library of Congress.*

nation's wartime president, were primed to swallow Dye's allegations hook, line and sinker.

Dye contended that the Slave Power's first attempt at getting rid of an unsympathetic president was in 1835, when it set up a mentally unstable housepainter named Richard Lawrence to shoot President Andrew Jackson in retaliation for Jackson's squashing of the nullification movement in South Carolina. That state's legislature, prompted by a federally imposed tax that it believed favored the North at the expense of the South, had passed a resolution declaring that the state had the right to nullify any act of the federal government contrary to local interests and sovereignty. Although a southerner himself, Jackson responded immediately and fiercely, promising to lead an army to South Carolina himself and hang the nullifiers, as the state legislators were called, from the nearest trees. Under this threat, a compromise, for which Henry Clay got most of the credit, was quickly worked out and the so-called Nullification Crisis was over.

One of the leading agitators for nullification was none other than Jackson's own vice president, South Carolinian John C. Calhoun, who resigned his Washington post to devote himself wholeheartedly to the cause of state sovereignty. Dye conceded that it was impossible to ascertain whether Lawrence, the unsuccessful assassin, acted alone or at the instigation of Calhoun, but he certainly insinuated a collaboration between the two. So far as Dye was concerned, Lawrence was acting under Calhoun's influence when, on January 30, he stepped up to Jackson as the president was leaving the Capitol and in quick order fired two pistols at him. The attempt failed because the powder in the pistols was too damp to ignite, and Lawrence spent the rest of his life in a mental asylum. The Slave Power, Dye concluded, had been thwarted only by the grace of God.

But not for long. The next two attempts at eliminating unsympathetic presidents succeeded all too well. According to Dye, the Slave Power resolved that President William Henry Harrison also had to go because he'd made it clear during the 1841 presidential campaign that he was unwilling to bring Texas into the Union as a slave state. So a month after his inauguration, when Harrison fell ill with pneumonia, someone in the pay of the Slave Power slipped the aged president small but escalating doses of arsenic sufficient to ensure his death. The official report from the Executive Mansion was that Harrison had succumbed to pneumonia. But eight days before his death, the president began vomiting and suffering from stomach cramps, which Dye concluded were clear signs of foul play. Given the abdominal distress suffered by the president in his final days, Dye posed this question (which, of course, was really a statement) to his readers: "Can anyone doubt that General Harrison was poisoned, and also that his physicians overlooked the true nature of the malady?"[61]

Harrison was succeeded by Virginian John Tyler, who immediately announced his support for the admission to the United States of the slave-holding Republic of Texas. So for the next four years, Southern powerbrokers were satisfied. Tyler was succeeded in turn by James K. Polk, who also, Dye insisted, was a pawn of the Slave Power. But trouble returned in 1848 with the election of Zachary Taylor to the presidency. Although a southern plantation owner, Taylor let it be known that he was willing to admit California to the Union as a free state, thereby upsetting the balance of power between slave and free states. "Those having slavery politically committed to their care," commented Dye, "had long before sworn that no person should ever occupy the Presidential Chair that opposed their schemes in the interest of slavery. *They resolved to take his life*."[62]

So they did, again by poison, administered to Taylor at a Fourth of July celebration in 1850. (Dye neglected to explain why the Slave Power waited for a full year and a half before killing the president.) The symptoms endured by Taylor in his death agony were similar to Harrison's nearly a decade earlier, which for Dye, clinched the case for assassination by poisoning. The

According to conspiracy theorist John Smith Dye, the Slave Power failed to assassinate Andrew Jackson but was more successful with Presidents William Henry Harrison (left) and Zachary Taylor (right). *Courtesy of the Library of Congress.*

fallen president was succeeded by Millard Fillmore, an "individual [who had] always been in favor of granting everything to slavery."[63] Once again, the Slave Power was appeased.

When Buchanan was elected to the presidency in 1856, he already had a reputation as a doughface Southern sympathizer. According to Dye, that wasn't enough for the "ultra pro-slavery men of the South," who "determined to control or kill him." The moment he stepped out of line, they resolved to get rid of him so that his Kentucky-born vice president, John Breckinridge, could succeed him. Their line of thinking, inferred Dye, was that "Buchanan *might* be sure, but Breckinridge *they knew* to be safe."[64] Breckinridge was from the South, he was a strong supporter of states' rights and he owned slaves.

What earned the president-elect the enmity of the Slave Power, Dye wrote, was the appointment of Michigan's Lewis Cass as Secretary of State. Cass was the politician who first proposed the doctrine of popular sovereignty as a solution to the vexing problem of slavery's westward expansion into the federal territories. This was too risky a strategy for the "ultra pro-slavery men." After all, people in the vast Kansas-Nebraska territories just might opt to ban slavery. So the minute they got word of the appointment, the fire-eaters made their move. Realizing that poisoning Buchanan in the same way they had murdered Presidents Harrison and Taylor would raise too many suspicions, they resolved, "to prevent investigation, a change of tactics…Instead of the President (as heretofore) being the only victim, it was so arranged that from twenty to fifty persons were to lose their lives, and among them President Buchanan. It would thus appear as an accidental occurrence."[65] Dye described the modus operandi of the assassination attempt by basically repeating a version of one of the crackpot theories that had circulated in the early months of 1857.

The plot was deep, and planned with skill. Mr. Buchanan, as is customary with men in his station, had a table, or chairs, reserved for him and his friends [in the National Hotel's dining room]. *The President was known to be an inveterate tea-drinker; in fact, Northern people rarely drink anything else in the evening. Southern men mostly prefer coffee. Thus, to make sure of Buchanan, and cause as many deaths in the North as possible, arsenic was sprinkled in the sugar bowls containing the tea or lump sugar, and set on the table where he was to sit. The pulverized sugar used for coffee sitting on the table was kept free from the poisonous drug by deep-laid strategy; thus, not a single Southern man was affected. Fifty or sixty persons dined at different intervals at that table that evening; and as near as we can ascertain about thirty-eight died from the effects of the poison.*[66]

Dye got his dates wrong, claiming that Buchanan and his friends first fell ill in late February instead of late January, and contrary to his claim, some Southerners, in particular the fiery states' right champion John Quitman of Mississippi, indeed did fall ill. But he wrote in such a confident manner that many of his readers trusted his account. Moreover, Dye insisted that Dr. Foltz, Buchanan's physician, as well as Buchanan himself, was under no illusion about what had happened. Foltz, claimed Dye, saved Buchanan's life by immediately treating him for poisoning. For his part, Buchanan, "intimidated by the attempted assassination, became more than ever the tool of the Slave Power."[67] Throughout the rest of his administration, he would favor policies that promoted the interests of the South and the expansion of slavery in the Kansas Territory, and Dye was convinced that this was a direct consequence of his near death at the hands of the Slave Power.

THE ABOLITIONIST CONSPIRACY

At the opposite end of the spectrum from Dye's speculations about the National Hotel outbreak was a charge levelled by Rose O'Neale Greenhow, one of the most remarkable women of her generation. Buchanan's would-be assassins, she contended, far from being slave-holding Southerners, were actually Northern abolitionists. Their motive for doing the president-elect in was his perceived sympathy for the South. Greenhow didn't come right out and name members of the fledgling Republican Party as the plot's instigators, but it was clear that she considered them part of the "Abolition party" at which she *did* point a finger.

Greenhow grew up on a small Maryland plantation, situated between Baltimore and Washington, D.C. Her father died when she was one or two years old (the date of her birth is unclear), and the bulk of his estate, including fifteen slaves, was sold to pay off his many debts. Her widowed mother, left virtually penniless, sent young Rose and one of her sisters to be properly raised by an aunt in the nation's capital.

Rose did well there, learning the skills that a future society lady needed. By the time she was twenty-one, she had married handsomely—her husband, Dr. Robert Greenhow, was a rising diplomat in the State Department—and she

Rose O'Neale Greenhow, the Confederate secret agent who claimed that abolitionists conspired to murder Buchanan in order to instigate a war against slavery. *Courtesy of the Library of Congress.*

was a regular of Dolley Madison's circle. By 1850, when her husband was sent on diplomatic missions to Mexico City and San Francisco, the Greenhows had become one of Washington's best-known society families. Mrs. Greenhow, an avid student of politics, was well acquainted with many of the congressional luminaries of her day, including James Buchanan. She was especially impressed by South Carolina senator John C. Calhoun, the great champion of nullification, whom she called "my kindest and best friend."[68]

After only four years in San Francisco, Dr. Greenhow was killed in an accident. His widow returned east and settled in Washington, D.C., residing for a while in Brown's Hotel, not far from the National. After a period of mourning, her interest in politics gradually revived. As the presidential election of 1856 approached, she wrote her old friend Buchanan, by then serving in London as ambassador to the Court of Saint James, entreating him to throw his hat in the ring because he was the only man capable of defeating the Black Republican candidate John C. Frémont. If the Republicans won the White House, she predicted, the Union would likely split apart over the issue of slavery. "The country at this moment is in a state of revolution. People have, in all ages, held it as their sacred right to resort to revolution when the evils of government could not be amended in any other way."[69]

Mrs. Greenhow's defense of the "sacred right to revolution" wasn't just rhetoric on her part. When the country finally divided following the election of Abraham Lincoln, the first Republican president, she unhesitatingly

South Carolinian John Calhoun, whose ardent defense of southern states' rights was admired by Rose Greenhow. *Courtesy of the Library of Congress.*

endorsed the rebellious Confederacy and its championship of slavery. Given her standing in Washington society, she was well situated to hear information that could help the Confederate war effort, and she was quickly recruited to spy for the newly formed Southern nation. Her handler taught her a coded script with which to convey messages. She used it in the summer of 1861 to relay to the Confederacy Union battle plans and troop movements for what became the First Battle of Bull Run. President Jefferson Davis later attributed the defeat of General Irvin McDowell's army to Greenhow's intelligence-gathering. This may have been too generous an assessment. But it's undoubtable that Greenhow's spy work contributed to the Confederate victory.

Greenhow's career as a secret agent was short-lived. Federal officials arrested her shortly after First Bull Run. Although held for nearly a year, she was never brought to trial, probably because she was a widowed mother and President Lincoln wished to avoid the scandal of a public inquiry. In May 1862, Greenhow was released into the custody of Confederate officials and warned never to return north. One year later, she eluded the Union blockade of Southern ports to travel to England as an emissary for the Confederacy. It was during her time abroad that she published a memoir of her adventures, *My Imprisonment and the First Year of Abolition Rule at Washington,* in which she told of "the appalling attempt of the 'Abolition party' to poison President Buchanan, the chiefs of the Democratic party, in Washington, at the National Hotel, a few days prior to the inauguration of President Buchanan."[70] The book became something of a sensation among British readers.

As Greenhow tells the story, the miasma explanation for the National Hotel outbreak was a smokescreen to hide what really happened. According to her, Caleb Cushing, the attorney general of Buchanan's predecessor Franklin Pierce, had received a letter from a Philadelphia druggist informing him that someone from Washington had ordered thirty pounds of arsenic. An unknown person had picked up the arsenic in the capital city. Quite understandably, Cushing hadn't acted on this information, since at the time no crime appeared to have been committed with the purchased arsenic. But Greenhow alleged that this was the poison used on Buchanan and his fellow Democrats at the National Hotel, and that the person in charge of Buchanan's rooms there—a person who subsequently disappeared—was likely in on the plot.

In her memoir, Greenhow claimed that "a full and detailed account" of the plot was included among her private papers seized by the government when she was arrested. She also asserted that Jeremiah Black, Buchanan's attorney general, knew about the plot and wanted to go public with it, but that "Mr. Buchanan would not allow the affair to be pursued, because of the startling facts it would lay open to the world, and that he shrank from the terrible exposure."[71] In a rare criticism of her old friend, Greenhow noted that she "considered it a great weakness on [Buchanan's] part to have forbidden the investigation."[72] Had he not done so, public exposure of the length to which abolitionists were willing to go may have prevented the war.

But Greenhow's story is as unbelievable as Dye's. The detailed information she claimed to have about an abolitionist plot to murder Buchanan has never been discovered (she herself somewhat conveniently predicted that it would "never be brought to light"),[73] and it stretches credulity to imagine that any rational abolitionist would think that Buchanan's slave-owning vice president, John Breckinridge, would be a more acceptable president when it came to the issue of slavery. Predictably, Greenhow's account was greeted with disdain by the Northern press—the December 5, 1863 issue of the *New York Daily Times* savaged it as a concoction "as bitter as a woman's hate can make it"—while the Southern press generally lauded it. Mrs. Greenhow never backed away from the story. Her death one year after her book appeared—she drowned in the Atlantic while trying to return to the Confederacy—forever closed the door to any corroborating evidence she might have been able to produce.

The Jesuit Conspiracy

Anti–Roman Catholic bias has long been a stain on American history, stretching from colonial days to the present. One of the leading historians of American Catholicism isn't exaggerating when he bluntly writes, "a universal anti-Catholic bias was brought to Jamestown in 1607 and vigilantly cultivated in all the thirteen colonies."[74] The causes of the bias are complex, but two in particular stand out: a Reformation-inspired repudiation of what is seen as non-Biblical superstition and ritual and political distrust of a religion whose members, charge critics, swear their first allegiance to the Vatican instead of the country in which they dwell. In addition, the hierarchical nature of the Roman Catholic Church is often viewed as contrary to the American spirit of democracy.

Beginning in the mid-nineteenth century, with the influx of huge numbers of Roman Catholic German and Irish immigrants, anti-Catholicism became intertwined with the exclusionary nativism that characterized the short-lived Know-Nothing Party and then, after the Civil War, the Ku Klux Klan. Anti-Catholic potboilers that titillated readers with lurid accounts of over-sexed nuns and lecherous priests became popular. One in particular, published in 1886 by an excommunicated priest named Charles Chiniquy, especially appealed. Titled *50 Years in the Roman Church*, the book is a long-winded indictment of Roman Catholicism that rehashes all the charges of corruption, superstition and political intrigue that are the stock-in-trade of such literature. But what made the book a must-read for thrill-seeking readers was the charge, tucked away in a couple chapters toward the end, that Jesuits had plotted and carried out Abraham Lincoln's assassination. Their motive? Lincoln had secretly converted to Roman Catholicism earlier in life, had later apostatized and so had to be punished for his infidelity. In describing the alleged conspiracy, Chiniquy allowed that Southern interests financed the plot but insisted that it was instigated by Roman Catholics. How else to explain the fact, he asked, that both the assassin, John Wilkes Booth, and all the tried and convicted conspirators were Catholics? (They weren't, by the way.)

Chiniquy's accusations were bizarre, but they proved popular with a certain element in the American public—his book, in fact, is still in print today—and it inspired another book, published in 1922, that not only repeated his claim that the Jesuits had murdered Lincoln but also did him one better. Burke McCarty, author of *The Suppressed Truth about the Assassination of Abraham Lincoln*, argued that Jesuits had also murdered two earlier presidents, William Henry Harrison and Zachary Taylor, and had tried to kill a third, James Buchanan.

According to McCarty, who described herself as an "ex-Romanist," the pope, frightened by the French Revolution, had entered into an unholy alliance with the monarchs of Europe to overthrow democracies whenever and wherever they happened to appear on the globe. The arm of the Church best suited to carry out this intention was the Jesuit order, which had a long history, McCarty contended, of making "the BIG IDEA of democracy, taught by Jesus Christ,…the target of their venom."[75] Moreover, McCarty claimed, all Jesuits took a solemn and secret oath to employ whatever foul means necessary to carry out their mission. "I will secretly use," her upper-cased rendering of the oath read,

THE POISON CUP, THE STRANGULATION CORD, THE STEEL OF THE POINARD, OR THE LEADEN BULLET, REGARDLESS OF THE HONOR, RANK, DIGNITY OR AUTHORITY OF THE PERSON OR PERSONS WHATSOEVER MAY BE THEIR CONDITION IN LIFE, EITHER PUBLIC OR PRIVATE, AS I AT ANY TIME MAY BE DIRECTED SO TO DO BY ANY AGENT OF THE POPE OR SUPERIOR OF THE BROTHERHOOD OF THE HOLY FAITH OF THE SOCIETY OF JESUS.[76]

The bloodthirsty oath was sheer fabrication, of course, the imaginative invention of a Masonic invective against the Catholic Church that McCarty uncritically quoted. But it served as the foundation for her charge that Jesuits had conspired to kill Buchanan. Given their hatred of freedom and democracy, both the Vatican and the European monarchical powers, argued McCarty, had long supported the American South's "peculiar institution." Harrison and Taylor had to go because they exhibited signs of refusing to allow slaveholders the run of the continent, thereby displaying dangerous democratic tendencies. Buchanan's doughface reputation initially made him seem a safe choice. But just to be on the safe side, shortly after his election, "Southern leaders got in touch with him with the intention of testing him out." By that time, Buchanan, intimidated by "the rumble of the Abolitionists' wheels," had backed away from his pro-South position and "coolly informed" his visitors "that he was President of the North, as well as of the South."[77] This was too much to be tolerated, and so arsenic, the same poison that had killed Buchanan's two predecessors, was administered to Buchanan at the National Hotel. The assassination attempt failed. But "the close call to death frightened and made James Buchanan the most subservient tool the Jesuits"—and, presumably, the South—"ever had."[78]

McCarty's book, absurd as it is, likewise remains in print to this day.

A LAST WORD

The diehard conspiracy buff might still object that it's impossible to prove that the National Hotel disease was caused by backed-up sewage instead of a plot to murder Buchanan. The only reply that can be given this challenge is "yes...but." It *is* impossible to prove the sewage hypothesis beyond any shadow of doubt. Moreover, given the heated political climate of early 1857, there were certainly Americans north and south of the Mason-Dixon Line who despised the president-elect and who would have gladly seen him out of the picture. Finally, some of the outbreak's details—its containment within a single building in the capital city, the judgment of some medical authorities that its symptoms indicated poisoning and the odd coincidence that it struck during both of the president-elect's visits to the National—clearly lent themselves to speculations that human agency was at work. One could reasonably dismiss the wilder conspiracy theories without necessarily rejecting the possibility of some kind of plot to murder Buchanan.

But on the other hand, there's an absence of credible evidence to suggest that the events at the National Hotel were the consequences of an assassination plot. The conspiracy theories that emerged were for the most part speculative and fast and loose with the actual facts of the outbreak. At the end of the day, there was no smoking gun, no chain of evidence and no compelling explanation of motive. Moreover, the preponderance of physical evidence—the frozen backup of sewage ditches followed by sudden thawing in late January and early March; the noticeably foul odor in parts of the National; the fact that most of the hotel staff, and especially the kitchen workers, also sickened; the only slightly contested testimony that the people who were stricken had eaten at the National; and the failure of inspection teams to find any signs of deliberate or accidental poisoning—strongly suggests that the most probable explanation of the National Hotel disease was that it was an outbreak of some form of cholera caused by sewage contamination. When it comes to historical explanations, probability is the best that can be hoped for.

Even though the most likely explanation for the outbreak at the National Hotel was medical rather than conspiratorial, the very fact that Buchanan's illness was almost immediately rumored to be the consequence of an assassination attempt, and that this possibility kept the nation enthralled for half a year, is a revealing barometer of just how fragile the country's equilibrium was after a decade of intense and increasingly fraught debate about slavery. The sectional distrust and dislike generated by the debate created a toxic breeding ground for the politics of paranoia. In early 1857, the paranoia expressed itself in fear that either the president-elect had been poisoned at the National Hotel or that an insidious disease had erupted there that, for all anyone knew, was likely to spread far and wide throughout the land. When the animosity between North and South finally erupted in full-scale war four years later, perceptive observers, thinking back to the paranoid days of 1857, might well have seen them as a portent of far worse things to come.

PERIOD COVERAGE OF THE NATIONAL HOTEL DISEASE

FROM *SCIENTIFIC AMERICAN* 12, NO. 29 (MARCH 28, 1857)

"The National Hotel Sickness"

A great many versions of the origin of the sickness which of late has affected the guests at the National Hotel, in Washington, have been given, but none that we know of which accord with the opinions of those who have been upon the spot and taken the pains to inquire into the facts. The rat poisoning is something which occurred two or three years ago, and the story has probably been re-hashed now because the stench or odor about some parts of the house seems to resemble that then observed.

The proprietors of the house, like the few boarders who adhere to it through evil as well as through good report, are utterly ignorant of the cause of the disease, while they are not, and cannot be blind to the fact of its existence. Like others, they can only conjecture, while they hope it may speedily pass away. Their continued ignorance of the cause does not speak well, however, for their energy. They have satisfied themselves with proving that it does not come either from the food or the water, and there they stop, having in despair closed the house.

The fact that the poison is in the air is proven not less by the investigations into food and water, than by the unpleasant odor which pervades the lower stories, and the existence of water-closets in various parts of these stories, while there is neither odor nor water-closets in the upper stories, points to them and the sewage pipes as the probable causes of the difficulty.

Learning wisdom by experience, President Buchanan, on his late visit to Washington, previous to his inauguration, took up his lodgings, privately, at the residence of Mr. Corcoran, the banker, while at the same time he retained his rooms at the National, occupying them only during the day, and venturing to eat nothing save a cracker during lunch. Visitors at the National can be "spotted" in many parts of the country, simply by the disease, which, if it did not attack them while in Washington, followed them to their homes.

In character, the disorder closely resembles the lighter forms of cholera.

FROM THE *BROOKLYN CIRCULAR* (APRIL 2, 1857)

"Sickness at the National Hotel in Washington"

For several weeks past the newspapers have given accounts of a distressing endemic disease affecting the guests and employees of the National Hotel, in the City of Washington. The symptoms of the disease were diarrhea, of an unusual kind, and sometimes vomiting, great thirst, &c. It is stated that not less than one thousand persons have been more or less affected with the disorder since its first appearance, which was in the latter part of January. Mr. Buchanan, the newly elected President, has been one of the sufferers. Having come to Washington previous to his inauguration, and put up at the National, he was attacked with the disease, and was in consequence compelled, as was said, to return suddenly to his home in Pennsylvania. He had not fully recovered from its effects at the time of his inauguration—if indeed he has at the present date. In two or three cases the disease has proved fatal. As to its cause, current report has ascribed it to the poisoning of rats, and by means of them the water of the hotel. The statement was, that the proprietors of the hotel had used strychnine, or arsenic, to destroy the rats; that the effect of the poison on the animals was to make them seek water; and that great numbers of them got into the water-tanks of the hotel and died, thus poisoning the water that was used for cooking, &c. A different account of the matter, however, has been given in a recent letter from the Mayor of Washington to the Board of Aldermen and the Common Council of the City, in connection with the report of a committee appointed by the Washington Board of Health to examine into the cause of the disease referred to. The committee, referring to the testimony of the physicians whom they had examined in relation to the character and causes of the disease, say:

> *There was no evidence, in the opinion of these gentlemen, of anything like mineral poisoning having been taken into the stomach: there was no evidence of inflammation of the intestines. They concur in regarding the disease as one of "blood poison," produced by the inhalation of a poisonous miasm [sic], generated by animal and vegetable decomposition, which entered the hotel through the sewer connecting with the Sixth-street sewer. The Committee sought in vain for evidence of the water or food having been poisoned by arsenic or any other mineral substance. Drs. J.C. Hall and C. Boyle both state that they drank the water—Dr. Hall says, "freely, without being affected by it."*

The Mayor expresses his concurrence with the conclusions arrived at by the committee, believing them true. In reference to the faulty construction of the hotel, he says:

> *The hotel was not built upon any pre-conceived and well-arranged plan, but has been several times extended and otherwise altered, so that it has been impossible to adopt or carry out any regular system of ventilation. Indeed that object, important as it is, seems to have been almost entirely lost sight of, and with many of the old flues, with their registers, placed in the building to conduct the heated air through it, have been suffered to remain, though the method of heating the house has been changed; and they serve as conduits through which mephitic [pestilential] gases were conveyed all over the house.*

In addition to the above, it is stated that the sewers of the hotel are now undergoing remodeling and reconstruction, and it is confidently that with the changes contemplated, the house will be rendered healthful and salubrious.

FROM THE NEW YORK DAILY TIMES (MAY 2, 1857)

"The National Hotel Mystery"

It is full time that the mystery of the National Hotel disease should be made the subject of judicial investigation. No proved atrocity could be so alarming as the shrugs and innuendoes flying like poisoned arrows through the dark; no false respect for individual interests can longer be permitted to suppress the inquiries that have now become essential to public tranquility, the national honor and, perhaps, the security of the life of our Executive. Through the paper that has always been regarded as his own home organ, Mr. Buchanan confesses his suspicion of foul play; and after a confirmation of this kind from the quarter least likely to exaggerate such a doubt, our public rumors have intensified into positive charges, and the dark cloud that rested over Washington has taken the precise outline and tangibility of a vast conspiracy to murder.

"There are certain coincidences connected with this subject," says the *Pennsylvanian*, "which are suggestive of the most horrible suspicions; but for the honor of human nature we hope they are unfounded." And it then goes on, in its guarded and semi-official way, to recite "coincidences" that have never yet received the requisite attention. A "hope" is, by no means, the right weapon for the defense of "the honor of human nature"; and hopes of the kind here faltered, by suggesting enormities beyond the reach of our experience, only serve to serve a blacker doubt over the dark records of proved and attested depravity.

The "coincidences" are indeed extremely curious, and, whether fortuitous or criminal, present a chain of circumstantial evidence that could have been left unfollowed in no other city of the civilized world than Washington alone. The air of our federal capital seems to emasculate the moral nerves; and crimes have been committed there, and quietly hushed up, or triflingly disposed of, that would have raised a thunder-storm if transpiring in any less exalted region.

But now for the coincidences to which, through his own home organ, our Executive seems anxious to direct attention. Mr. Buchanan arrived at the National Hotel, Washington, on the 25th of last January. Next day the first case appeared of a new and strange disorder—the symptoms, violent purging, inflammation of the larger intestines and a swollen tongue; giving all the indications of some poison of a mineral nature. Guest after guest was taken down with precisely similar symptoms; and within two days thirty-five of the inmates were so ill as to be confined to bed, and numbers—the President-elect amongst them—were taken dangerously sick, either previous to, or immediately after leaving Washington.

From the date of Mr. Buchanan's departure for Wheatland—where he arrived greatly altered and enfeebled—not one single new case of the disease occurred until after his return to the hotel on the 2nd of March: but on the day of the inauguration, this strange disorder reappeared with exaggerated virulence and a wider sweep—seven hundred guests or upwards being attacked together, and of these some twenty-five or thirty have since died of its lingering and recurring agonies. The remedies, where successfully employed, were for the most part of the nature of mineral antidotes; and where the disease was treated as one of miasmatic origin, we find the sufferings more protracted, and the mortal issue involved of greater doubt.

It has been publicly stated in various reputable papers, and the statement remains uncontradicted to this hour, that "the President received a letter warning him not to partake of food at the National. If so," adds the *Albany Argus*, "here is evidence of a crime, and perhaps a clue to its discovery. Why is it not pursued?"

But is not this letter a fabrication designed to round off a parallel that is otherwise complete? Can it be possible that the Chief Magistrate should have received such a letter and yet—even after its dreadful confirmation—persist in taking no legal notice of the monstrous conspiracy to which it might serve as a clue? We would dismiss the supposition as incredible, were it not for the strong language used ("the symptoms uniformly indicating poison") in the paper which, of all others, should be most conversant with Mr. Buchanan's opinion. The *Pennsylvanian*, while giving its official endorsement to the "horrible suspicions," has not one word to say about the letter; and silence in a case of this kind, is, at least, as significant as words.

The disease broke out on Mr. Buchanan's first visit; the disease disappeared on Mr. Buchanan's departure; the disease returned again with Mr. Buchanan, as if it were a shadow that dogged his heels; and Mr. Buchanan is said to have received a letter announcing that danger lay in wait for him at the very house where a disease, from which he has not yet recovered—from which he may never recover—overtook and pulled him down. The disease was confined, not only to *one* house in a crowded city, but to such of the frequenters of that house as partook of *food* within its walls; the disease presented the same diagnostics in every case, whereas all other epidemics that we know of are modified in different cases by the physical idiosyncrasies of the individuals attacked; the disease presented all the symptoms usually resultant in cases of mineral poisoning, and its victims, though scattered to the four climates of the Union, undergo frequent and wasting relapses—a thing not consonant with our experience of miasmatic exhalations, but tending directly to prove that the poison, of whatever kind, is carried *in them* and has laid fast hold of their systems.

So much for the "coincidences," which we put forward without deducing any theory.

From the National Era (May 7, 1857)

"The National Hotel Disease–Fatal Cases"

Some time since, after a mysterious disease had prevailed for months at the National Hotel in this city, until the house was almost deserted, the Board of Health instituted an investigation into the nature of the malady and its causes. The mischief had already been done; the causes had probably ceased to exist; nothing or little remained to be done, even in the way of prevention. Had the Board noted in time, it might have thrown some light upon the mystery, but its tardy investigation and report were alike useless. It could find nothing deleterious but bad sewerage—the sewers were so constructed that unwholesome vapors found their way into the building, and produced the dreadful disease! All this seemed to us like trifling with the community. There is no doubt that we are afflicted with bad sewerage in more places than the National Hotel, and unwholesome gases, too, but they do not produce a chronic and virulent disease of the mucous membrane of the bowels, running on for months, and in some cases terminating fatally.

Mr. Buchanan came to Washington in January or February, spent a few days at the National, contracted the disorder, and has suffered from paroxysms of it ever since. Mr. Hale boarded there, was seized by the demon, and has not yet got rid of it. Hundreds of cases there are of the same kind. Change of air and place works no cure. The malady, whatever it is, goes with the victim wherever he goes, and gnaws at his vitals. Sometimes, he thinks himself well—but in a little while, pain, distention of the bowels, copious diarrhea and prostration, admonish him that the lurking poison is still there.

The Board of Health, in their report, said that no death had then resulted from it. Dr. Antisell, in a paper read before the National Institute of Washington, April 18, said, "I believe there is no direct case in which a fatal result followed." It is perhaps true there is no case in which death has directly or speedily followed the first attack of the disease—but that it has proved fatal in protracted cases, cannot be denied. Only the other day, we saw recorded the death of Mr. Montgomery, of Pennsylvania, who had carried the malady with him from Washington; and the statement is made, that a post-mortem examination revealed in the mucous membrane of stomach and bowels all the indications of the workings of poison.

Dr. Antisell, in his paper, examines the various hypotheses about sewerage, mephitic gases, miasma, &c. and demonstrates, we think, their absurdity. He abandons, too, his own theory at first entertained about the disproportionate amount of salts in the water used, as the cause of the endemic. Nor does he believe that it was the result of poison taken through the food or water. On this point, we think his remarks unsatisfactory. His examination and experiments were entirely too limited to authorize any positive opinion one way or the other. There may have been poison, and yet it may not have been present on the day or days when he made his investigations. The manner in which the disease affected the system; its protracted action; the occasional abatement of the symptoms and then their violent renewal; the appearance on post-mortem examination; and the absence of any other assignable cause, naturally awaken the suspicion that poison in food or drink may have been at the bottom of the mischief. And yet, on this hypothesis, it seems difficult to explain why all were not affected, and why some have suffered who stayed at the Hotel, and took their meals elsewhere.

If the supposition, however, should prove true, it does not follow that the poisoning was intentional. The suspicion is too monstrous to be for a moment entertained. It may have resulted from causes beyond the knowledge of the proprietors and servants. Dr. Antisell tells us in his paper that in the kitchen he "found the utensils bright and clean, the coppers all free from oxidizement, but *not perfectly tinned*"—to this last circumstance, however, we attach no consequence. Now, we confess, that so much do we detest copper, we will not have it used in cooking, so long as cooks are what they are—and we should feel in some trepidation, if we should learn that we had been eating solids or liquids from copper stew-pans or boilers, not perfectly tinned. We would trust nothing to the cleanliness or carefulness of cooks or their helpers. If they used copper, not well tinned, they would be sure now and then to serve up enough of the oxide to do mischief.

We throw out these considerations, not because we have a definite, well-grounded opinion as to the cause of the fearful endemic, but because we do not think the examinations instituted in relation to it, were commenced early enough, or conducted thoroughly enough.

From the *New York Daily Herald* (May 8, 1857)

"The National Hotel Disease"

The Academy of Medicine, we think, the other evening gave the quietus to the enormous humbug that the late National Hotel disease at Washington was the result of a dastardly attempt to poison Mr. Buchanan. The stinking sewers, venting their deadly exhalations into and all over the house, will, or ought to, account for the malady and solve the mystery to the satisfaction of all sensible people. That any human being could entertain such a diabolical and venomous hatred of Mr. Buchanan as to risk his death by poison, involving the lives of hundreds of unoffending people—men, women and children—passes all bounds of credulity. We have no doubt that Mr. Buchanan, in his election as President, and since, has had fewer enemies and more universally the good wishes of all parties and all sorts of men than any other President since the time of Monroe. These are the natural fruits of his well-known amiable, kind and conciliatory character as a man and as a politician. We suspect that this poisoning humbug is the weak invention of some disappointed office beggar, or some of the Washington hotel keepers, and nothing more.

From the *New York Daily Times* (May 8, 1857)

"The National Hotel Disease"
A Letter to the Editor

The first account I received of the extraordinary disease at the "National," was from a gentleman who had been employed as steward or head waiter in the hotel. At the time he communicated the information, he was in the employ of Mr. Murray, at whose house I was boarding. He said a large number of persons were sick; that Dr. Hall was overwhelmed with business; that the hotel was *poisoned,* and that people would find out it was poisoned. Having many friends at the National, I enquired particularly his authority for such statements. He said he had been employed at the "d—d place," and that he had just left it because it was nothing but a hospital, which no one could remain in in safety. He then indulged in a perfect torrent of abuse of the proprietors; his invective was personal and continual, and he never failed to improve an opportunity to urge a boarder to leave the hotel, or to prevent a stranger entering it. His regular and extraordinary abuse of the proprietors, whom I had always found to be as gentlemanly and courteous as any men with whom I had ever had any intercourse, satisfied me that there had been some misunderstanding, and that his charges were prompted by no motive short of the gratification of personal revenge.

Having, in conjunction with a large number of friends, spent a portion of almost every evening of several weeks at the National—having drank the water almost as regularly as that of any other hotel in the place, and believing it next to impossible for anything like a plague to break out in the middle of Winter, I did not credit the ex-steward's statements, but was surprised to find, a short time after he had made them, that several of my friends, who had been in the city but a little while, were already suffering severely from sickness, which they had contracted after their arrival.

(signed) G.P. Buell

FROM THE *NEW YORK DAILY TIMES* (MAY 15 1857)

"The National Hotel Disease"
Two Letters to the Editor

Sir: As there much interest evinced by the public in the origin of the "National Hotel disease," I deem it the duty of every one to throw all the light in their power upon the matter, and to correct any statement they may detect error in. I notice in the letter of your Washington correspondent "Uno," in this morning's *Times*, he says: "To establish the fact beyond doubt that this disease proceeded from the malaria at the hotel and not poison, Mr. Buchanan, when at the hotel, neither ate nor drank there." It is conceded that the first symptoms of the disease in Mr. Buchanan made their appearance while he was at the National, in the latter part of January: he arrived on the 27th. I was at the hotel when he arrived, and breakfasted at the same table with him. I also saw him at dinner twice that week at the ladies' ordinary. The rooms he occupied at that time were Nos. 15 and 16, in the west wing on the corner of Sixth and C streets, second story above the street; that is the wing in which your correspondent of this morning, "J.D.," speaks of noticing "a deadly and disagreeable smell." The middle of December I arrived at the National, and occupied the rooms alluded to with my wife; both of us noticed the peculiar close and nauseating smell, particularly on entering the hall in the morning. On the third day after our arrival I was taken with the disease, and have been dangerously ill with it until a month since, when I for the first time got relief, and trust I am now free from it.

As to the suggestion that the slaves in the establishment poisoned the food or water, I would remark that all the servants were white, and during the past two years I have not seen a black on the premises, save one old man, whose station was in the water closet. There may have been some employed in the cooking department, but my impression is that they were all white. The proprietors can easily set that hypothesis at rest.

I would further remark in order to settle the question as to the date of the appearance of the disease, that I knew five or six gentlemen who were suffering under it when I was taken (about the 15th December).

(signed) R.

Sir: I have read a letter in your issue yesterday from a victim of the "National Hotel sickness," who thinks it was produced by poisoning with arsenic.

He states that, while at the Hotel, he became unwell on the 22nd of April, and hastened home, where, on the 25th, he became much worse and sent for an homeopathic physician, who pronounced his symptoms those of poisoning by arsenic, and cured him with homeopathic doses of iron!

From his own history of his case, it seems highly improbable that arsenic could have produced his illness, or that he could have received any benefit from the treatment to which he resorted. The best authorities on the subject state, that the worst effects of a poisonous dose of arsenic are produced within twenty-four hours after it is swallowed. Hence, if his sickness had been produced by arsenic taken into his system at the National Hotel, the acute symptoms of which he complained would have come on within a few hours after he left there and not at the end of three or four days after his return home.

It is quite improbable that he received any benefit from the treatment to which he resorted; for under any circumstances homeopathic doses of iron must prove useless as an antidote for arsenic; nor could any dose be of service after the poison had found its way into the circulation.

(signed) W. Argyle Watson

FROM THE *OHIO MEDICAL AND SURGICAL JOURNAL* 9, NO. 6 (JULY 1, 1857)

"The National Hotel Endemic"
A Letter to Dr. C. Boyle

In answer to your queries concerning the endemic disease at the National hotel, I have to state that my observations were limited to but two cases, and these yielded to the simplest anodyne treatment.

Although a member of the board of health, I was not one of the investigating committee; yet, at a previous meeting of the board, I distinctly indicated to them that probably the sewerage of the hotel was at fault. One of the proprietors had called upon me, before I had heard of the existing disease, and, after the most careful questioning, I could learn nothing from him but that one of the water closets had exploded when a lighted paper was accidentally cast into it. He then gave me the names of the persons who purveyed for the hotel, which showed that the food used was the same as that furnished for the tables of a large proportion of the community. The drinking water supplied to the house was analyzed, and with no other results than that there was some slight excess of saline ingredients. If the fault was there, why were not you and the thousands in that vicinity who used the same water daily, similarly affected? You know, however, that there were no cases outside of the house.

The board of health was informed that the sewerage of the hotel was not perfect, and the fall to the canal in which it drained, was very trifling. The intensity of cold during the past winter was almost unprecedented, and the canal into which the sewers emptied was almost frozen solid. It must be remembered that if the main or corporation sewer was perfectly pervious, still the private sewer, which had so little fall, was probably not so. Of this, though, we must judge from the effects.

The disease, I learn, began during the intense cold weather, in a house which always has been thought to be badly ventilated, and, if you remember, all the piazzas which surround its court yard were tightly closed with glass. No particular alarm was at first created; and it even seems that every endeavor was made to stifle every noise in regard to the matter, as everyone supposed that the affair was but of a temporary character. The board of health, however, was informed and learned that a peculiar diarrhea did exist, and that it was on the decline. The attempt then made to attribute the malady to the spring water used was promptly repudiated by the board, and its opinion was inclined to the imperfect ventilation and sewerage. The members of the board for that ward visited the premises, according to their obligation. At this time the weather moderated, the house was well ventilated [because windows were thrown open], and no source of offensive or noxious exhalation could be found. A subsequent visit of the commissioner of health led to the same result; and therefore a card was published, stating that after a careful examination of the premises, no local cause of danger was manifest.

[An official investigatory] committee was [formed and] ordered to inspect the premises thoroughly, and to take testimony. This they did do, and with the greatest promptitude, on account of the great anxiety of the public mind. The testimony taken before them, as well as the examinations made, induced them to reiterate the opinion that they believed the malady to be due to imperfect sewerage. The waste water drains and those from the privies emptied into a sewer which, from its trifling fall and the want of a "stench trap" on the premises, cast the noxious exhalations from the offensive matters into the house, and more especially at night, when there was less ventilation and motion in it. Numerous witnesses were examined as to the mode of their attack, &c., and it was found that some had suffered who had neither eaten nor drank in the house. The cooks were violently attacked, and with relapses of the greatest severity. Mr. Gaultier, the chief cook, who prepared the whole of his private food, appears to have been the greatest sufferer of all. The servants of the house were constantly sick, so that the attendance on the sick guests was necessarily bad.

On carefully inspecting the premises, some of the investigating committee were rendered sick by the smell in certain portions of the house, and more especially in a room which contained a hot air register, long unused, and which communicated with the cellar. Whilst attending a patient there for another disease, I had noticed a very offensive or putrid odor in portions of the house. Of course, before the committee paid their sanitary visit to the premises, preparations could have been easily made to cleanse and sweeten the house, and therefore any unhealthy or filthy condition be removed. I was informed that during the cold weather a water closet above the pantry (which was between the ordinaries) had overflowed, and the said pantry was exceedingly offensive. I was also informed that the closet used by the male servants of the house had been in a most disgusting condition during the severe weather. The exhalations from this cause, I was told, could also reach the pantry.

An examination of the sewerage was made by Mr. J.T. Ferry, a practical sewer builder, who witnessed with the committee that a stream of fetid gas poured from the sewer into the house with a sufficient force to extinguish a lighted candle.

FROM *SCIENTIFIC AMERICAN* 12, NO. 46 (JULY 25, 1857)

"The National Hotel Disease"

We have on several occasions presented facts as they successively appeared relating to the endemic at the National Hotel, last winter, and have remarked on the obviously great importance of a thorough understanding of its cause or causes, if possible. It is important to know how far slight exhalations in the atmosphere may affect health, and cases are very rarely presented so important in themselves as the one in question. The official report of the section of the New York Academy of Medicine on Theory and Practice and Medical Pathology, presented to that body at their last meeting a report in which they unanimously adopted the "foul air" theory. They set forth that the source was solely a poisonous atmosphere, probably engendered in the receptacles for offal and other filth, under the building or adjacent thereto, in the sewers, &c., these having been obstructed by ice or otherwise by neglect, until the accumulation of foul air and noxious gases involved the atmosphere in and around the building, and, as in other cases of malarial exhalation, severely and dangerously affecting its inmates.

The foul air, the report presents, is the one common cause, which exposed all who inhaled it a predisposition to the malady, which itself was modified in individual cases by previous health, and developed with greater or less promptness and severity by excesses, or indiscretions in diet, drink, exposure, &c., either of which might have been harmlessly indulged but for the universal predisposition induced by the atmospheric poison. And, in like manner, even the predisposition, as in other cases, was not followed by an attack in all such, because no exciting cause was applied of sufficient potency. And again, many who received this predisposition had no symptom of the malady until days or weeks after they had left the atmosphere of Washington and returned to their homes. Then, under some exciting cause, the disease was developed, their predisposition having remained latent meanwhile. These cases the report contends have been sufficiently numerous all over the country, and so well characterized as to be identified as originating at Washington by unequivocal pathognomic [*sic*] symptoms.

This view of the subject is unanimously believed to explain many of the circumstances reported by authority as marking the endemic, and which are wholly inconsistent with any theory of mineral poison. For example, while some persons sickened after a single drink taken at the bar, there were many others who ate, drank and slept exclusively in the hotel, throughout the whole endemic, without a single symptom. There were, besides, numbers who suffered an attack who nseither ate nor drank in the house, but only visited it, or mayhap slept there. Yet it is remarkable that no case of the disease is alleged by anybody in which the patient had not been in the hotel and inhaled the air. This common cause, the poisoned atmosphere, having been present in all cases, while none of the other causes are known to have been present in many and all are known to be absent in others, seems to render the conclusion rational and philosophical. And as it is illogical to seek for more causes for any effect than are necessary for its production, the physicians signing the report are not willing to admit any other poison than that which the foul air of the hotel furnished as the common cause of all the endemic visitation which has been suffered by our Washington neighbors; and they commend to the civic authorities there and everywhere the sanitary lesson taught by this pestilential endemic.

Let none of them henceforth ignore the facts here exemplified, and at whatever season of the year filth is allowed to accumulate to an extent sufficient to pollute the atmosphere of any inhabited house, the health and lives are endangered, not merely of its inmates, but of its neighborhood, by the privation of pure air for lack of ventilation, no less than by the noxious and poisonous quality of the infected atmosphere itself.

FROM THE NEW HAMPSHIRE JOURNAL OF MEDICINE 7, NO. 8 (1857)

"The National Hotel Disease"
Letter from Isaac O. Barnes

Dear Sir—You ask me for a statement of such facts as came within my knowledge, during my recent illness at the National Hotel, in the city of Washington, and since my return this spring, having reference to the somewhat peculiar disease, which, last winter, seems to have invaded and depopulated that ill-fated house.

I comply very cheerfully with your request, because you are pleased to say, that by some possibility, which I really believe must be very remote, such a statement may do good hereafter, to somebody; although I cannot but believe that everybody in the whole community has already been treated to the facts and to speculations, theories and conjectures *usque ad nauseam* [to a disgusting extent], upon this literally sickening subject.

I took lodgings at that hotel on the morning of Friday, the 30th day of last January, and had my meals there regularly during that and the following day. The third day I dined elsewhere, but returned in the evening to the hotel. During the night of this third day I was attacked with diarrhea, but not very violently, having been compelled to leave my bed, I think, only twice. Upon saying something about my illness, the next morning, to some friends and fellow-lodgers, I found, somewhat to my surprise, that a great number of the inmates of the establishment were in the same unpleasant condition with myself; in fact everybody about me was complaining of similar difficulty and derangements.

All this, however, occasioned no alarm or panic, for no one of the whole number seemed to consider himself very seriously ill. Nobody, so far as I know or heard or believe, had then applied, or even thought of applying, for medical advice. I had not, nor did not then, nor for five days afterwards; and there were five or six gentlemen, with whom I spent most of the time for the four succeeding days, all of whom were as unwell as myself, who did not call in the aid of any physician. To show you how trivial and unimportant all considered this disease, in its inchoate state, I may mention that I happened to be in a room with some ten or a dozen gentlemen, one of whom was Mr. Buchanan, the then President-elect, who had himself been seized with it; and I remember distinctly that he and others remarked, that it seemed so mild in its character, one might anticipate a salutary and beneficial result to the general health rather than any evil consequences from its presence. A day or two after this, as there seemed to be no abatement of the disease, several of us applied to a neighboring apothecary and were furnished with some astringent preparation, said to be a specific for such troubles, and we were temporarily relieved...

One peculiarity, to my mind, in this disease, has been *an entire absence of pain,* from its commencement to its ending. I have never felt the slightest sensation of pain in the region of the stomach, nor in any part of what, I think, you call the great vital package, nor in the lower viscera, nor in any other part of my body, which could, in any manner, or by any possibility, arise from the action of this disease, from its first inception to the moment of this writing; and my own experience in this particular is the same as that of at least thirty others, with whom I have compared notes. One gentleman, adverting to this peculiarity, remarked to me that he thought it an altogether ugly symptom, and that he should be rejoiced to experience some sort of pain—colic pain—any pain, any sensation except that which seemed to be upon all of us—a very death-like torpor of the whole viscera, upper and lower.

The fecal discharges in my case, and in all with which I was acquainted, were most copious, uniformly watery, frothy and of a peculiar unnatural, acrid smell; in appearance as all agreed, like so much baker's yeast. These dejections were so abundant, expelled with such tremendous force, so entirely overwhelming, so extravagant and disproportionate to the quantity of food taken into the stomach in a given time, as to stagger belief, and to become as frightful as they were exhausting to the patient. We were all annoyed immeasurably with flatulence, with the abdomen strained to a drumhead tension and with a sickening, disgusting, swill-like acidity of the stomach.

Unnatural *thirst* was another accompaniment. I have seen a statement in some newspaper, which declares that we all hankered after acidulated drinks. I can't speak for other parties, but what I desired, longed for, prayed for, dreamed of and thought of, day and night, was what, of course, I could not have—some good, pure, cold water from our own New England wells. A dreadful *nausea* has been, in my case, the very worst and most miserable attendant upon this complaint. I have felt it almost all of the time, from the first till now. If I were, even today, to take an ounce of beefsteak, or that amount of any animal food into my stomach, my experience thus far is, that I should suffer for hours from this horrid nausea.

There is one other feature of this calamitous sickness, which seems to merit the attention of the medical profession; and that is its probable regular *intermittent* character. It recurred quite regularly, in my case, during the first five or six weeks, once in about three days. Since that time, the intervals between the attacks have been weaker and weaker as time has progressed. All agree that this regular and constant recurrence, again and again, after the patient had reason to suppose himself cured, is as strange and unusual, as it is discouraging and disheartening to the party who suffers. So far as my experience goes, I can bear witness that it has been the source of most intense and terrible suffering.

NOTES

Chapter I

1. Lincoln, *Collected Works*, 385.
2. Smith, *Magnificent Missourian*, 313.
3. Klein, *President James Buchanan: A Biography*, 257.
4. Walther, *The Shattering of the Union: America in the 1850s*, 91.
5. Baker, *James Buchanan*, 72–73.
6. Stamp, *America in 1857: A Nation on the Brink*, 6.
7. Ibid., 7.
8. Klein, *James Buchanan*, 262.

Chapter II

9. Adams, *The Education of Henry Adams*, 759.
10. Froncek, *The City of Washington: An Illustrated History*, 177.
11. Trollope, *North America*, 304.
12. Gugliotta, *Freedom's Cap*, 26.
13. Froncek, *The City of Washington*, 141.
14. Ibid., 176.
15. de Tocqueville, *Democracy in America*, 469.
16. Furgurson, *Freedom Rising: Washington in the Civil War*, 14.

17. Winkle, *Lincoln's Citadel: The Civil War in Washington, D.C.*, 3.

18. Furgurson, *Freedom Rising*, 14.

19. Abdy, *Journal of a Residence and Tour of the United States of America*, 98.

20. Borchert, *Alley Life in Washington: Family, Community, Religion, and Folklife in the City, 1850–1970*, 19.

21. Green, *Washington: A History of the Capital, 1800–1950*, 215.

22. Ibid., 217.

23. Winkle, *Lincoln's Citadel*, 123.

24. Gugliotta, *Freedom's Cap*, 27.

25. Winkle, *Lincoln's Citadel*, 124.

26. Ibid., 123.

27. Haley, *Philp's Washington Described: A Complete View of the American Capital, and the District of Columbia*, 207.

28. Ibid.

29. DeFerrari, *Historic Restaurants of Washington, D.C.*, 52.

30. *Brooklyn Circular*, April 2, 1857.

31. Pitch, *"They Have Killed Papa Dead!": The Road to Ford's Theatre, Abraham Lincoln's Murder, and the Rage for Vengeance*, 54.

CHAPTER III

32. Curtis, *The Life of James Buchanan*, 188.

33. Stamp, *America in 1857*, 59.

34. *Washington Evening Star*, January 26, 1857.

35. Foltz, *Surgeon of the Seas: The Life of Surgeon General Jonathan M. Foltz*, 181.

36. Ibid.

37. Klein, *James Buchanan*, 267.

38. Foltz, *Surgeon of the Seas*, 182.

39. Ibid.

40. Nichols, *The Disruption of American Democracy*, 89.

41. Klein, *James Buchanan*, 211.

42. Foltz, *Surgeon of the Seas*, 187.

43. Smith, *The Presidency of James Buchanan*, 23.

44. Klein, *James Buchanan*, 241.

45. Ibid., 239.

46. Lincoln, *Collected Works*, 2:495.

47. Horton, *The Life and Public Services of James Buchanan*, 440.

CHAPTER IV

48. Barnes, "The National Hotel Disease: Letter to Dr. D.H. Storer," 241.
49. Waring, "National Hotel Endemic: Autopsy; with Remarks," 104.
50. Ogle, *All the Modern Conveniences: American Household Plumbing, 1840–1890*, 57.
51. *Fayetteville Observer*, March 26, 1857.
52. Reid, *Ventilation in American Dwellings*, 92.
53. Barnes, "The National Hotel Disease," 243.
54. "The National Hotel Sickness," *Scientific American* 12 (January 1857): 230.
55. Ibid.
56. Ibid., 365.
57. Barnes, "The National Hotel Disease," 238.

CHAPTER V

58. Richard Hofstadter, "The Paranoid Style in American Politics."
59. Ibid.
60. "Slavery and the Slave Power in the United States of America," 17.
61. Dye, *The Adder's Den; or Secrets of the Great Conspiracy to Overthrow Liberty in America*, 41.
62. Ibid., 52.
63. Ibid., 55.
64. Ibid., 84, 90.
65. Ibid., 90.
66. Ibid., 91–92.
67. Ibid., 94.
68. Blackman, *Wild Rose: Rose O'Neale Greenhow, Civil War Spy*, 141.
69. Ibid., 171.
70. Greenhow, *My Imprisonment and the First Year of Abolition Rule at Washington*, 41.
71. Ibid., 42.
72. Ibid.
73. Ibid., 41.
74. Ellis, *American Catholicism*, 19.
75. McCarty, *The Suppressed Truth About the Assassination of Abraham Lincoln*, 16.
76. Ibid., 23.
77. Ibid., 59
78. Ibid., 61.

BIBLIOGRAPHY

Abdy, Edward S. *Journal of a Residence and Tour of the United States of America*. Volume 2. London: John Murray, 1835.

Adams, Henry. *The Education of Henry Adams*. In *Henry Adams: Novels, Mont Saint Michel, The Education*. ed. Ernest Samuels. New York: Library of America, 1983.

Baker, Jean H. *James Buchanan*. New York: Henry Holt, 2002.

Barnes, Isaac O. "The National Hotel Disease: Letter to Dr. D.H. Storer." *New Hampshire Journal of Medicine* 7 (1857): 238–243.

Blackman, Ann. *Wild Rose: Rose O'Neale Greenhow, Civil War Spy*. New York: Random House, 2005.

Borchert, James. *Alley Life in Washington: Family, Community, Religion, and Folklife in the City, 1850–1970*. Urbana: University of Illinois Press, 1980.

Curtis, George Ticknor. *The Life of James Buchanan*. Volume 2. New York: Harper and Brothers, 1883.

DeFerrari, John. *Historic Restaurants of Washington, D.C.* Charleston, SC: The History Press, 2013.

de Tocqueville, Alexis. *Democracy in America*. ed. J.P. Mayer. New York: Harper Perennial, 1988.

Dye, John Smith. *The Adder's Den; or Secrets of the Great Conspiracy to Overthrow Liberty in America*. New York: Published by the author, 1864.

Ellis, John Tracy. *American Catholicism*. Chicago, IL: University of Chicago Press, 1969.

Foltz, Charles S. *Surgeon of the Seas: The Life of Surgeon General Jonathan M. Foltz.* Indianapolis, IN: Bobbs-Merrill, 1931.

Froncek, Thomas, ed. *The City of Washington: An Illustrated History.* New York: Alfred A. Knopf, 1985.

Furgurson, Ernest B. *Freedom Rising: Washington in the Civil War.* New York: Vintage, 2004.

Green, Constance McLaughlin. *Washington: A History of the Capital, 1800–1950.* Volume 1. Princeton, NJ: Princeton University Press, 1962.

Greenhow, Mrs. Rose. *My Imprisonment and the First Year of Abolition Rule at Washington.* London: Richard Bentley, 1863.

Gugliotta, Guy. *Freedom's Cap: The United States Capitol and the Coming of the Civil War.* New York: Hill and Wang, 2012.

Haley, William D'Arcy. *Philp's Washington Described: A Complete View of the American Capital, and the District of Columbia.* Washington, D.C.: Philp & Solomons, 1860.

Hofstadter, Richard "The Paranoid Style in American Politics." *Harper's Magazine* (1964). http://harpers.org/archive/1964/11/the-paranoid-style-in-american-politics/.

Horton, R.G. *The Life and Public Services of James Buchanan.* New York: Derby & Jackson, 1857.

Klein, Philip S. *President James Buchanan: A Biography.* Newtown, CT: American Political Biography Press, 1962.

Lincoln, Abraham. *Collected Works.* ed. Roy Basler. Volume 2. New Brunswick, NJ: Rutgers University Press, 1953.

McCarty, Burke. *The Suppressed Truth About the Assassination of Abraham Lincoln.* Washington, D.C.: Burke McCarty, 1922.

"The National Hotel Disease." *Scientific American* 12 (July 1857): 365.

"The National Hotel Sickness." *Scientific American* 12 (January 1857): 230.

Nichols, Roy Franklin. *The Disruption of American Democracy.* New York: Collier, 1962.

Ogle, Maureen. *All the Modern Conveniences: American Household Plumbing, 1840–1890.* Baltimore, MD: Johns Hopkins University Press, 1996.

Pitch, Anthony S. *"They Have Killed Papa Dead!": The Road to Ford's Theatre, Abraham Lincoln's Murder, and the Rage for Vengeance.* Hanover, NH: Steerforth Press, 2008.

Reid, David Boswell. *Ventilation in American Dwellings.* New York: Wiley & Halstead, 1858.

"Slavery and the Slave Power in the United States of America." *Blackwood's Magazine* 73, no. 447 (January 1853): 17.

Smith, Elbert B. *Magnificent Missourian*. Philadelphia, PA: Lippincott, 1958.
————. *The Presidency of James Buchanan*. Lawrence: University Press of Kansas, 1980.
Stamp, Kenneth. *America in 1857: A Nation on the Brink*. New York: Oxford University Press, 1990.
Trollope, Anthony. *North America*. New York: Alfred A. Knopf, 1951.
Walther, Eric H. *The Shattering of the Union: America in the 1850s*. Lanham, MD: SR Books, 2004.
Waring, James J. "National Hotel Endemic: Autopsy; with Remarks." *American Journal of the Medical Sciences* 35 (January 1858): 98–104.
Winkle, Kenneth J. *Lincoln's Citadel: The Civil War in Washington, D.C.* New York: W.W. Norton, 2013.

PERIOD NEWSPAPERS AND JOURNALS CONSULTED

American Journal of the Medical Sciences
American Publishers' Circular and Literary Gazette
Baltimore Sun
Blackwood's Magazine
Boston Daily
Brooklyn Circular
Brooklyn Eagle
Cincinnati Commercial
Columbus Enquirer
Fayetteville Observer
Harper's Weekly
Lancaster Evening Express
Lancaster Inland Daily
Lowell Daily Citizen
Maine Farmer
National Era
New Hampshire Journal of Medicine
New York Daily Herald
New York Daily Times
Ohio Medical and Surgical Journal
Pennsylvanian
Pittsfield Sun
Scientific American
Washington Evening Star
Weekly Wisconsin Patriot

INDEX

ABOUT THE AUTHOR

Kerry Walters received his PhD from the University of Cincinnati. He has been a professor at Gettysburg College for over twenty-five years and is the William Bittinger Professor of Philosophy. Walters is the author of thirty-five books on philosophy and theology, and he has published several books on the Civil War. His first book with The History Press was *Explosion on the Potomac: The 1844 Calamity Aboard the USS* Princeton.

Visit us at
www.historypress.net
....
This title is also available as an e-book